THE
ADOLESCENT
DIARIES
OF
Karen Horney

THE ADOLESCENT DIARIES

OF

Karen Horney

Basic Books, Inc., Publishers

NEW YORK

All photographs are from the collection of Renate Horney Patterson.

Library of Congress Cataloging in Publication Data

Horney, Karen, 1885–1952.
   The adolescent diaries of Karen Horney.

   1. Horney, Karen, 1885–1952. 2. Psycho-
analysts—United States—Biography. I. Title.
RC339.52.H67A3   616.89′00924   80–50552
ISBN: 0–465–00055–X

CONTENTS

Foreword by Marianne Horney Eckardt, M.D.

[vii]

First Diary

1899–1900

[3]

Second Diary

1900–1902

[17]

Third Diary

1903–1904

[55]

Fourth Diary

1904–1907

[87]

[v]

CONTENTS

Letters

to Oskar Horney

1906–1907

[163]

Fifth Diary

1910–1911

[237]

FOREWORD

THESE DIARIES were discovered after Karen Horney's
death in 1952. Out of respect for the privacy she always
cherished, they were not examined closely at that time.
By happenstance they remained in the possession of
Karen Horney's youngest daughter, Renate, and gathered
dust in her bookshelf for twenty years. Then one day
Renate, who had emigrated to Mexico from Germany in
the late thirties, was sitting in her living room, looking
past the tiled patio into her luscious garden of bougain-
villas, musing. Her mind turned to a tale about buried
treasure in her garden. This was not a new line of thought,
since she had absorbed much Mexican folklore and was
by temperament inclined to believe in the more mysterious
forces that shape our destinies. Where could this treasure
be? Her eye fell on five slim volumes in a large bookcase,
the five diaries of her mother. Immediately she knew this
was the treasure. She took them off the shelf and read
them with growing absorption. Her mission took form:
with care, she transcribed the neatly handwritten docu-
ments; the English translation saw many revisions, the
main credit going to Mrs. Crena de Iongh. Renate's eldest
sister, Brigitte, helped to fill in a large gap by unearthing a
bundle of letters written by Karen Horney to her future
husband, Oskar, which Brigitte had been given by Oskar
Horney's second wife after his death.

The diaries required very little editing. Only a few entries
were omitted in consideration for the flow of the narrative.
While the diaries that follow speak for themselves, a few
facts describing the family, its setting, and some highlights of Karen's career may help to locate the reader.

Karen's father, Berndt Wackels Danielsen, was born in Bergen, Norway, and rose to be Commodore (or sea captain) for the Hamburg America Line. He became a German national and settled in Hamburg. His first wife died, leaving him with four teen-age children. Three years later he married Clothilde Van Ronzelen, Karen's mother, who was seventeen years his junior. The children of the first marriage never accepted their new stepmother or their stepsiblings.

Clothilde's father, of Dutch descent, was an engineer-architect famous for his construction of the port facilities in Bremerhaven. He had three wives. Clothilde's mother, his second wife, died when giving birth to Clothilde, who was then raised, together with children from the first marriage, by the third wife. It was a warm family. Clothilde, called Sonni, was beautiful and commanded attention. She married Wackels when she was twenty-seven years old. Their son Berndt was born in 1881, and their daughter Karen in 1885. Karen's father was fifty years old when she was born. Thus Karen grew up in a good middle-class home. The diaries suggest a rather typical home, steeped in conventional prejudices of class, religion, and race.

Karen Horney's lively discourse with herself ends in 1911. Only a few highlights of her remarkable career will be mentioned. She became a psychiatrist and psychoanalyst. In 1917 her first scientific paper, entitled "The Technique of Psychoanalytic Therapy," initiated her rich scientific discourse. She began to grapple with Freudian doctrine in her early papers on feminine psychology, as she recognized the cultural bias in Freud's male-centered construct of the libido theory. She emigrated to the United States in 1932. Moving from one society to another reinforced her awareness of the importance of cultural factors in personality development. This led to her first book, *The Neurotic Personality of Our Time* (1937). Her second book, *New Ways in Psychoanalysis,* debated Freud's major concepts and cleared the deck for her own ideas. Each of the subsequent books—*Self-Analysis* (1942), *Our Inner Conflicts* (1945), and *Neurosis and Human Growth* (1950)—brought forward the progression of her own conceptual system. After her marriage dissolved in 1926, her writing—the search for the truth—became her passion. She worked with intensity and devotion and was deeply unhappy when she felt unproductive even for short periods of time. She died of cancer in 1952 at the age of sixty-eight.

In our present struggles for women's rights, Karen Horney appears to be a pioneer. The facts place her in the vanguard throughout her life. She attended the gymnasium within a short time after it became available for women. In Hamburg women were first permitted in the gymnasium in 1901. The universities of Baden, Freiburg, and Heidelberg were the first to accept women into their medical schools—in 1900. The medical school of the University of Berlin did not open its doors to women until 1908. Psychoanalysis was introduced to Berlin in 1908, and Karen Horney was just a medical student when she began psychoanalytic therapy in 1910 with the only practicing psychoanalyst of that city, Dr. Karl Abraham. Yet, there is a sense in which Karen Horney was not just a fighter for women's rights. A simpler and more remarkable situation existed: she had an unquestioned sense of her own intellectual gifts and superiority, and an unerring sense of her own destiny. This the world affirmed and her diaries demonstrate.

Marianne Horney Eckardt, M.D.

First Diary

1899–1900

SONNI, BERNDT,
AND KAREN

COMMODORE BERNDT
WACKELS DANIELSEN

〰〰〰〰〰〰〰〰〰〰〰〰〰〰〰〰〰〰〰〰〰〰〰〰〰〰〰〰〰〰〰〰〰〰〰〰〰

Hamburg, 7 June 1899

How I come to be writing a diary is easy to explain: it's because I am enthusiastic about everything new, and I have decided now to carry this through so that in later years I can better remember the days of my youth.

Now, for a short introduction, the following: we, i.e., Mother, Berndt, who is now 17 years old, and I, live in Eilbeck, Pragerstrasse to be precise. My best friends are Tuti and Käthe. We are in the second class at the Convent School. Our favorite teacher is Herr Schulze; he teaches our German lessons, history, and religion. Unfortunately he is sick now and lives in Reinbeck, where we plan to visit him on Sunday: that is, Mother with Tuti and me. Last year we had German with Frl. Schöne, whom Tuti and I were also crazy about, though we like Herr Schulze much better still, because the way he treats us is so charming. Our homeroom teacher is Frl. Friendländer. Dr. Dietrich teaches arithmetic, chemistry, and geography. I am excused from technical subjects at my doctor's wish. I was very glad about this too, since I am very clumsy at drawing and needlework. Outside of school I have piano lessons and gym. As we now get up at 6:30, I had a chance to practice piano for ½ hour today before school. And today we had a surprise in school: Dr. Dietrich, who has been in military training since the Whitsuntide holidays, was back. I am not quite sure whether I am glad about this or not, but really, the many classes with substitute teachers are always so dreary. Herr Schulze will be away until summer vacation. Anyway, Thursday is *not* my favorite day, for in the first place we have gym, which I don't like because I'm always afraid Frl. Banning, the gym teacher, will find fault with me for something or other, since I am not exactly a star in gymnastics and conduct. And secondly, Thursday we have German grammar!

I feel very dignified today, since I had my hair pinned up for the first time even though I am only 13 years old. In spiritual matters I still feel *very unworthy*, for although I am steadily growing up, I do not yet feel the true need for religion. A sermon can overwhelm me and at times I can act accordingly, but prayer. . . . The need—spiritual poverty—in a word: the thoughts. Unfortunately I have to stop now, it is bedtime.

May God kindly help me.

8 June 1899

The great event in school today was that we were photographed. Frl. Schöne stood in front of me, Dr. Dietrich sat beside me. I don't really know whether I'm glad about the second fact. In French class Frau Zimmermann was absent, so I had to pay close attention. That isn't as easy as I thought.

Today Herr Dr. Dietrich was—I don't really know— either charming or awful. He had us freezing with open windows. Thank God I got an "A" on my English homework. If only it were already tomorrow. The train leaves here at 9:18 and at 2:30 we are back in Hamburg. I am just back from gym where, since our leading gymnast was absent, I had to take her place.

12 June 1899

It was *heavenly* yesterday. On the drive to the station we met Frl. Banning and had a very nice conversation with her. On the road to Reinbeck we picked flowers for "him," poppies, camomile, and pretty weeds. When we arrived in Reinbeck, he was not home yet, but 5 minutes later he came. Oh, that feeling, as he stepped into the room! What bliss to look into his beautiful eyes. I believe I won't forget that moment very easily. He shook our hands again and again, saying: "Dear children." He, too, has great respect for Pastor von Rückteshell, our splendid minister in Eilbeck, and we now know where he usually sits: up in the choir loft, though we'll have to find out whether to the left or to the right. We both believe we may conclude from a few words of his that he will invite us sometime. Oh, how lovely that would be! In the afternoon I went to Tuti. Nothing special happened in school today.

14 June 1899

Just had my piano lesson. These theory exercises are really terrible. Herr Schmidt was quite nice. Ah!! Herr Schulze!! I work with Tuti on her French almost every day since she is very weak in this subject.

15 June 1899

Oh, these substitute teachers. Today we saw a sample of our class photograph. Very nice. —*Das Ewige Licht* is a most beautiful book.* I am very much looking forward to the sea. We are going to Langballigau, a little village on the Baltic Sea. I hope I can take my diary along, if not, I'll catch up later. I really would not like anyone to read it. In 8½ weeks Herr Schulze will be back, then vacation is over.

16 June 1899

Today is a very beautiful day. I got an "A" on my French test and, what is better still, Tuti also got an "A," for the first time, I believe. To you, my diary, I will confide that I have sent Herr Schulze 6 bottles of wine. On the package label I wrote: *Sender*, "From someone who has the sincerest wish to see you well soon." Today we are to write a composition about Schiller's "Cranes of Ibycus." I rather like doing it. Käthe has just been here. She told me about Lisbeth H. She is the stupidest and worst in our class. She has got herself all snarled up in lies and bad behavior, poor child. How sorry I am for her.

19 June 1899

Tuti and I went to see Anita M. on Sunday. She is a darling little girl, so earnest and so selfless. I can learn a lot from

---

* *The Eternal Light*, a novel by Peter Rosegger. [Ed.]

her. After school we went for a nice swim in the Alster-
bach, except the water was dirty. This morning I got a
picture postcard from Berndt, signed by some of the
senior class, from Chabeutz, where they made a trip on
Saturday. We are going to go on our school excursion to
Geesthorst tomorrow. Alas, without Herr Schulze! How is
that possible? I don't believe that we will be able to go
tomorrow because of the weather. For 4 weeks the weather
has been fine, but tomorrow? It's thundering and lightning
right now.

21 June 1899

The trip yesterday was fine. Naturally it would have been
a thousand times nicer with Herr Schulze. But Herr Dietrich
was very jolly. The steamer trip was perfectly beautiful.

28 June 1899

Herr Schmidt, my piano teacher, gets more amiable every
day. There's a bone of contention between Tuti and me:
Lisbeth H. She is too limited to know any sense of tact.
Tuti is always too harsh with her, and then I feel morally
obligated to protect her. That makes Tuti angry with me.
I am really very sorry for Lisbeth: I act according to, "What
Jesus has given me is worthy of love."

5 July 1899

Yesterday was an eventful day. To begin with, Herr Schulze was back. Everybody brought him flowers. He lives in Reinbeck and left at 12 o'clock yesterday. Käthe and I had no classes and so we asked him if we might carry the flowers to the station for him. And we did. It was heavenly. I believe he will invite Tuti and me some day.

7 July 1899

We are leaving tomorrow morning. The trunks are already packed. My being away from school for 4 days is very hard for me, as Herr Schulze is back. Today my thoughts lingered alternately on him and in Langballigau, our destination. Yesterday I had a card from Erna B. She is one of those about whom I think a great deal. I am truly fond of her. She is a deep, thinking human being, and since, as she says, I understand her, she has often told me that she likes me. She has a gift for rhyme and poetry, and sometimes produces very nice things, but she is too silent. She always speaks or writes in an elevated style. She loves to play the piano and plays it well. I also got a card from Erik, a "Karl May"* card: very nice. My friend Erik is a lively boy but pretty scatterbrained. I am very much looking forward to tomorrow. Farewell, my diary, there is no room left for you in my trunk. Farewell.

---

* Karl May, author of her favorite adventure stories of American Indians and the Wild West. [Ed.]

1899–1900

29 July 1899

We came home yesterday. The trip went well. It was quite nice there. Swimming grand, only I couldn't swim for a week because I had influenza. A very nice Doctor Dugge took care of me. Once when we were taking a walk he told me a whole lot of things about the study of medicine. Now I see my goal to study medicine more clearly before me. First years of splendid but strenuous work, then being able to serve mankind through curing diseases. When I was younger, it was the large amount of money I would then possess that attracted me, now it's something else, something more precious. I read the *Kampf um Rom* ["Battle for Rome"], a grand book that deals with the battles and the downfall of the Goths. Splendid characters appear in it.

Frau Schmidt, our laundress, had my bird "Männi" as a boarder; she brought him to me today, but when I saw him, it wasn't my Männi but another siskin. She had let mine fly away. I have been reading with interest for a theme of my own choice on "The Preliminaries of Legislation," which pleases me very much. Now I still have two weeks' vacation and am longing terribly for school, for Herr Schulze, Tuti, and Käthe.

1 August 1899

Today Berndt went back to school for the first time. If only I could take his place. Yesterday we climbed the "Tyrolese Mountains" (in the amusement park). Now people are even building mountains. It is magnificent. It is supposed to remain 5 years, the "Mountain Trip in the Tyrol." And how far along will I be in 5 years? In the Gymnasium?

10 *August 1899*

Lots of fine things have happened. For one, Mother has written to Hannover to ask for a prospectus for the Gymnasium there, where I could take a teacher's examination. That would already be a certain step toward my plans for the future. We haven't received it yet. Secondly, Mother and I visited Herr Schulze in Reinbeck and made a wonderful (through his personality) trip to Aumühle with him. Five weeks from the day after tomorrow is my birthday, on which Berndt and I are to give a big mixed party. Today we go to Berndt's girl-friend's for supper. Yesterday we went to the Fährhaus to hear a concert. Recently to the Zoological Garden. Only 4 more days and school begins again. My little siskin is sweeter than the other one. He can't fly yet.

15 *August 1899*

Have had 2 splendid days. Seeing everybody again was wonderful. Herr Schulze was delightful, all lessons fine, the prospectus has come, Lisbeth H. is not coming back, fortunately for her and for us, and Herr Schmidt still won't be back tomorrow—what more could one want? I got only "B+" for my essay, which makes me pretty mad, but nobody got an "A" and that consoles me somewhat. Herr Schulze said today that he wanted to invite Anita, Tuti, and me this Sunday or next.

1899–1900

22 August 1899

Sunday we were in Reinbeck. It was lovely, just like Paradise. Tomorrow Herr Schulze is going to make another class trip with us to Silk near Reinbeck. It is heavenly.

24 August 1899

Yesterday we made a lovely class trip to Venttorf. At the station I sat opposite Herr Schulze, then I carried his coat, which I enjoyed very much. On our way there Anita and I walked alone, in Venttorf we met Susi Schulze* with whom we got on well. It's great in school. My favorite subjects are religion, history, chemistry, and French. I don't like arithmetic at all and the same goes for gym.

28 August 1899

Today is Goethe's 150th birthday. We had a very nice celebration in school.

30 September 1899

Today I got a bad mark for behavior. To be honest, it makes no difference to me whatever. It was because I let another girl copy. Otherwise it's really great in school.

---

* Herr Schulze's daughter. [Ed.]

[11]

This morning I got a sweet card from Susi Schulze. Tuti and I sent her one in return on which we are both photographed. Tomorrow we are performing "Prologue from the Maid of Orleans." Tuti is scheduled for confirmation instruction. That strikes me as very funny. It will soon be my birthday.

21 November 1900

My dear diary, I have been unfaithful to you. A whole year has gone by since I last confided a thought to you. But I'm afraid they aren't quite safe with you, because you have no lock. Oh, what *hasn't* happened in this year? From the fall of 1899 to the spring of 1900 my cousin Ada was with us. A very nice, good-natured, insignificant, rather lazy girl. We were in Lübeck for Christmas. My stepsister Agnes is now in Stockholm, teaching. On the third day of Christmas Tuti, Anita, and I were invited to Herr Schulze's where, it goes without saying, we had a heavenly time. We three had done a little piece of needlework for Susi Schulze and sent it to her in the morning. Tuti and I had a bitter quarrel about the wrapping. This was the first little rift in our friendship, but it unfortunately was to grow and finally become irreparable. Tuti is having confirmation lessons with a very liberal-minded minister, and she was herself very liberal-minded, while I was at that time rather narrow-minded in matters of faith. (I really had never reflected much about such things.) This put me off. Furthermore I was going to the theater a lot then and became somewhat dramatic under its spell. This in turn put her off. I can understand it now. In short, it finally came to a break, so that I didn't even go to her confirmation. I am sorry about this sometimes, for since then I haven't had a real friend, much as I long for one. Käthe does call herself my

friend, but she is too superficial for me, too coquettish—
especially since she has been taking dancing lessons. I'm
still passionately fond of going to the theater.

The summer of 1900 was the finest I've had so far, for we
were living in Reinbeck. The Schulzes had also moved
there and we were together many times. My adoration for
Herr Schulze established itself firmly. We went to school
together every morning. Our summer house was charm-
ingly situated. Our landlords were particularly nice. In
front of the house, meadows and woods, behind it the
Bille, a little stream where I could swim in good weather.
From time to time my girl-friends came to visit for a few
days. My friends Herman and Arnold also came often. But
this glorious life was to have a sudden end. In the beginning of September my stepsister Astrid, with her 5-year-old
daughter, came to stay for 5 weeks. She had behaved very
badly toward Mother in the past. Our idyllic life was over.
It went well enough so long as Father wasn't there, but
when he came in the end of September, all hell broke
loose, and up to now it has been getting worse rather than
better. Astrid incites him against mother. There are daily
scenes. It finally got so bad that Berndt and I didn't let
Mother out of our sight for a moment.

More another time, dear diary. There is an endless
amount still to tell. But now I just want quickly to shuffle
the cards for a game of Patience, before my father wakes
up. It is early morning, Day of Atonement. Mother is in
Lübeck, Berndt a-courting.

Second Diary

1900–1902

KAREN AT THE AGE OF TWELVE

〜〜〜〜〜〜〜〜〜〜〜〜〜〜〜〜〜〜〜〜〜〜〜〜〜〜〜〜〜〜〜〜〜〜〜〜〜〜

Hamburg, 24 December 1900

Christmas Eve is almost over. —The lights on the Christmas tree have burned down long ago. My beloved Mother is sitting with brother Berndt at the piano and was delighted with the songs Berndt got as a present. Father (today all bitterness is to be banned) is running from one thing to another and enjoying everything like a child, especially the goodies. Mother had the charming idea of surprising us with a genuine Norwegian *Julklap*. Even if the true (devout) Christmas joy won't enter my heart (I think back with a melancholy smile to the time—not yet so long ago— when I used to look forward to this fest for weeks), still I am really enjoying myself today. Mother has fulfilled all my wishes with her customary kindness. In addition to you, my dear Diary, I found a Negro boy (doll) that I had ardently longed for. I want to play with dolls again, although I'm already a 15-year-old *Backfisch** and am being "Sie'd"† in school. I also found a fine history book, but I

---

* Literally "a fish ready for the baking," an adolscent girl; the term may imply a little more of maturity, of the approach to woman-hood, than our term "teen-ager." [Ed.]

† Addressed with the formal "Sie" instead of the informal "Du." [Ed.]

want to exchange it for another more appropriate to my purpose. For the wars of liberation, which I would like to know more about, are treated here almost incidentally. I want to get a book on this subject recommended by my adored teacher, Herr Schulze. I was also very pleased with a dressing gown, material for summer dresses, a petticoat, a purse, gloves, a dish with sweets, a marzipantorte, effervescent powder, and a sweet little Delft lamp from Tante Clara. Unfortunately I was not able to finish my runner for Mother. But I will finish it in the next few days.

25 December 1900

Life is really pretty boring without school. I've been going to church in the mornings. Unfortunately this winter I will have to go whenever Pastor von Rückteschell preaches, because I am to be confirmed at Easter. My religion is in a desperately sad state at the moment. I am stirred by questions and doubts that probably no one can solve for me. Was and is Christ God? What is God? Is there resurrection? Is God personal? Is he a God of love? Confirmation lessons don't make it any clearer for me. I see this now with deep disappointment. Only the religion lessons with Herr Schulze, my idolized teacher, bring me some light. I really do admire him—with what interest, what patience and exertion he tries to allay my doubts. Thank God, school begins again a week from the day after tomorrow. I am sewing doll's things for my darling little Negro rascal, doing needlework, playing Patience, and reading.

26 December 1900

Mother is ill and unhappy. Alas, if only I could help my "dearest in the whole world." —How miserable you feel when you see your loved ones suffer. If only she is spared for Berndt and me, so that later on she can lead a friendly life with the two of us—when Berndt is a lawyer and I am a teacher. It is probably just as well that one cannot lift the veil of the future, and so can go on hoping. Yet I am always thinking of the future. How wishes and plans for later keep changing! Earlier, when I was still in private school, I did not think about the future at all. Then, when I went to the Convent School, I wanted to become a teacher. Then I went beyond that, and wanted to study. I wanted to go right away to the Gymnasium for girls, in my thoughts I was there already, but I had not taken Father into account. My "precious Father" forbade me any such plans once and for all. Of course, he can forbid me the Gymnasium, but the wish to study he cannot. My plan for the future is this:

1. Stay with Mother till Michaelmas, (i.e. 29 September) and then take my 1st exam.
2. From Michaelmas 1901 to Easter 1902 to Paris.
3. From Easter 1902 to 1905 to Wolfenbüttel.*
4. A couple of years as a teacher or tutor and preparing myself for final exams and medicine, on my own hook.
5. And ultimately: doctor.

You see, dear diary, Fate will have an easy time with me, for I prescribe everything for him.

But for the time being, I am still a student at the Convent School and am frightfully fond of going to school. We

---

* For training as a teacher. [Ed.]

really have awfully nice teachers, I'll describe their characters for you.

1. *Herr Schulze*, for history and religion. Heavenly, i.e., interesting, clever, quiet (almost imperturbable), naïve, liberal views, not petty, a little too exact and thorough, trusting (almost too much so), selfless, charming father and friend, lovable, ironic, interested in us, his pupils, kindly disposed, etc., etc. . . .

2. *Dr. Dietrich*, for geography and natural sciences. Treats us like recruits, rather rough, quite handsome, rather boring lessons, not pedantic and fussy, extremely unfair, outside school very jolly and nice, natural, vain, and severe.

3. *Dr. Karstens*, for German. Frl. Emmerich's favorite, moderately good lessons, fussy, strict, frightfully precise in correcting compositions, a hair-raising declaimer, but enjoys fine declamation, polite, fair.

4. *Frl. Banning*, for French (the ladies should have come first). Angelic, charming, interesting, clever, lovable, not strict, natural, opposite of pedantry and fussiness, unfortunately nervous, at times rather shy, delightful, like a sensitive plant (I believe it comes from nervousness).

5. *Frl. Emmerich*, class teacher for English. Very nice, clever, interesting, obliging, pretty fair, coquettish (with Dr. Karstens), trusting (rather too much), somewhat untidy, careless, the nicest classroom teacher one could imagine.

28 December 1900

Nothing came of the tour to Reinbeck: the weather was too bad and Mother feeling too miserable. Oh dear, if only we could move there.

It must be grand to have a father one can love and esteem, and when the 4th Commandment does not confront one like a terrifying specter with its "Thou shalt———." I can't do it. I can't respect that man who makes us all unhappy with his dreadful hypocrisy, selfishness, crudeness, and ill-breeding, etc.

I am exchanging my history book today for Beitzke's *Freiheitskriege* ["Wars of Independence"], three fat volumes only for the years 1813 to 1814. My mouth is watering already it's going to be such a pleasure. Afterwards I'm going to Käthe's to play with her puppet theater. I love everything connected with the stage, like: production, declamation, acting (in daily life not so much), costuming, puppet theater, etc. I believe I would go on the stage if I had more money and more talent. They do say I have talent for declamation and a good memory, but unfortunately I lack grace and singing talent.

30 December 1900

There is a party in the front room this evening. Herr Schulze is there too. How heavenly he is! I'm all ablaze in bright flames. I will wear my new dress, which he has admired very much.

31 December 1900

New Year's Eve, rather dreary. Mother and Berndt have gone to church. I can't help but think of last New Year's Eve. With how many good intentions, with what pious enthusiasm I went into the new year then. But now questions press upon me: what will 1901 bring us? The near future doesn't look any too brilliant. I look back at the past year with gratitude to God and man. But bitter self-reproaches press upon me too. Unkindness, lack of self-control, my unbelief, making fun of the holiest things, exaggerated enthusiasms, and serious offences against the 4th Commandment. For the New Year my resolutions are: 1. to stop mockery, even if I unfortunately don't possess a child's faith any more and no other faith has taken its place; 2. to learn to suppress my moods and tempers—to behave equably; 3. to try to fulfill the 4th Commandment at least outwardly. Today I read in a book that one should honor one's father not for his personal characteristics but to honor the authority God has vested in him. But it is awfully difficult.

3 January 1901

School began again today. School is the only true thing after all. It was heavenly. I was especially pleased by the fact that I got an "A" for my composition, and that Dr. Karstens declared it the best. The last days of vacation were very nice. At New Year's the master of the house was absent and a friend of Berndt's, Julius D., was there. We ate *Vielliebchen** together and agreed that the loser

---

* A childish custom in which, when breaking open almonds, peanuts, or the like, the person who gets the double kernel must recompense the other in some manner. [Ed.]

should take the others to the performance of *Don Carlos*. It is still not decided. Then I got a New Year greeting from "him," which made me insanely happy. He really is too divine. Last evening I saw Shakespeare's *Richard III*, a horrible play. But it was masterfully played. Tomorrow I have my first lesson since vacation with "him." I heard from one of the girls that she feels very unhappy in Wolfenbüttel. I'm curious to know if I will get there.

6 January 1901

Sunday . . . Brrr. . . . Berndt really is a fine fellow. Yesterday he again enlightened me on several things that were not clear to me. Up to now it has been the personality of Christ that was the most unclear. Although Herr Schulze has taught me about it, it seems to me to make no sense that Jesus should be God's son. Berndt told me: Christ is and always will be the greatest among all men, because the divine element, the thing that is embedded in every human being, was much stronger in him, and so he stood nearest to God. And he is here still (spiritually of course)— one has to think of resurrection in a spiritual sense anyway. —With this explanation a heavy burden fell from my heart, for I could not imagine, could not love, such a mixture of God and man. Now Jesus has become much dearer to me. —Then I heard from Anita, who is to be confirmed by Pastor N., that Christ's miracles were in part added in later writings and in part can be explained, for example, his healing of the sick through the power of his personality and the firm belief of the people in him. Something of the same sort has happened in this century too. Jesus does say himself that he can do no miracles in Nazareth because the people do not believe in him. Pastor

N.'s confirmation lessons must be very interesting. I wish ours weren't so horribly dull.

9 January 1901

Heavenly!! Heavenly!! Heavenly!! We're moving to Reinbeck, too marvelous. How glad I am. I'll tell "him" tomorrow. What will be the expression on his face? I go skating every day now.

10 January 1901

I'm furious at myself. No sooner am I happy about Reinbeck when another wish comes up in me, a burning desire. For in Hamburg a Gymnasium course is beginning at Easter, 4 or 5 years leading to the Arbitur.* I'd like to get there at Easter. Oh, wouldn't that be wonderful!! But Father. . . .

11 January 1901

Yesterday brought so much that was exciting and new that I couldn't sleep at all last night (which very seldom happens). Three of Mother's friends came one after the

---

* Arbitur is the final Gymnasium examination. [Ed.]

other yesterday, to work on Mother to send me to the Gymnasium. Mother spoke with Father afterward. He doesn't seem opposed to the matter itself, for him it's a question of money. So my chances have improved enormously. Beside that Berndt heard a lecture on "the woman question" by a gentleman who greatly praised the Gymnasium for girls. Berndt had to tell Father the whole lecture. When he goes to Tante Clara she will work on him too. Today Berndt is going to a lady who can inform us about admissions, age, courses, etc. I believe more and more that I "must" get there.

Then yesterday I heard a heavenly lecture by Anita's Pastor N., on the theme: "What meaning has the Old Testament for the Christian of today?"

12 January 1901

Something dreadful happened today. I'm afraid my adored Herr Schulze is angry with me. It happened this way: we were going through the 15th chapter of I Corinthians and so also through the (so-called) proofs Paul cites of Christ's resurrection, namely that he appeared to various people (after his death) and also to Paul. I dared to express the view that Paul had been in an overwrought nervous condition and so imagined he saw this luminous vision. I implied that this was really no proof of Christ's resurrection. I don't know if he misunderstood me or what, but in short, he got quite excited and said, slapping his Bible shut, that we could just as well busy ourselves with something else, anyone who didn't believe it could sit passively by for the time being, etc., etc. . . . and delivered a severe sermon to me. It is true he didn't address himself specifically to me, but of course it was meant for me. If I were not still totally dumbfounded, I should long ago have despaired, for the consciousness or the feeling that he is angry with me is terrible. I think I shall be very much embarrassed at his next lessons, for I cannot overcome this so easily.

My chances for the Gymnasium are getting better. I already know more about it. It's 5 years and begins with Oberteria [9th grade]. We don't need to know any Latin or mathematics. Once Father has digested the monstrous idea of sending his daughter to the Gymnasium, Mother will talk with him further. He is approachable now. I wanted to tell you my experiences only on Sundays, dear diary, but I experience so much every day that I just can't save it up till Sunday.

18 January 1901

This uncertainty makes me sick. Why can't Father make up his mind a little faster? He, who has flung out thousands for my stepbrother Enoch, who is both stupid and bad, first turns every additional penny he is to spend for me 10 times in his fingers. And we did make it clear to him that he has to feed me only as long as I attend school. Once I have my diploma I most certainly don't want another penny from him. He would like me to stay at home now, so we could dismiss our maid and I could do her work. He brings me almost to the point of cursing my good gifts.

19 January 1901

It's really true, at Easter I'm going to the Gymnasium. Father has just decided, when Mother handed him a document drawn up in verse, in which Mother and I promise that after I graduate he need do nothing for me. Oh, how happy I am!! And thankful!! First to the good Lord, for the fine gifts, then to Mother for her warm intercession and the way she handled it, then to Father for this permission!! Hurray!!

23 January 1901

Such is life [in English] . . . I am supposed to recite a dreadful, rumbling poem for the Emperor's birthday on Saturday. I've resisted as long as I could, but I must get at it; dreadful. Monday evening I went to the theater. It was grand and I had a heavenly time: 1. because the whole thing cost me only 65 pfennigs (I had gone to a standing-room area), 2. on account of the play, 3. on account of the nice company I met there (two brothers of my friend Olga). Before that I was at the Schulzes'. He wasn't there at first, but finally he came. I had wanted to tell him that I'm going to the Gymnasium. He was (of course) divine.

29 January 1901

So I did recite the poem on Saturday. Dr. Karstens hasn't said a word to me about it. I wonder if he was displeased with me? We had two lessons on Saturday before the celebration. In the second (religion) Frl. Banning practiced making a bow with me. She was charming. She is sweet to me anyway. Because I'm leaving at Easter and our class is way behind in French, she has me do extra work and explains all rules with the patience of an angel. Alas, my heart bleeds at the thought of having to lose her as well as Herr Schulze. Only 7½ weeks more. I have a good deal to do all the time: 1. the usual school work, 2. French work, 3. composition, 4. reading Karl May, 5. needlework, 6. really no work but fun—I tell myself stories all the time, now more than ever.

This story-telling is really awfully funny. I imagine what I would like to have. As chief characters appear my crushes and myself. The theme of the stories is similar, but each time I weave in whatever I have experienced or read. — Father is very hard to get on with now. He complains about everything, meals, clothes, behavior. Then he delivers conversion sermons, says endless, rather stupid, prayers every morning, etc. . . .

9 February 1901

I think I shall die of enthusiasm. Frl. Banning has been added to Herr Schulze. But she really is charming. For the last few days I have been taking my poetry album along to school, to have it inscribed by her. But I don't find the courage to ask her. I think I'll give it to "him" first. Finished a composition today. I am very glad of that, although it is terribly shabby. Composition is my weak side. The other subjects (except arithmetic) are getting awfully easy. Mother is now ill with influenza.

16 February 1901

Luckily Mother is better again. In any case, she's up. Herr Schulze inquires about her whenever he sees me. Ah, how divine he is. And now I only have 19 more lessons from him. This thought is dreadful to me. He is delightful to me. Recently I almost lost Frl. Banning's love for me. On Saturday she told us to write in class a composition either on "L'histoire de Bambam" or on "La distribution des Prix." But I had left my exercise book at home. As this was the second time that it had happened, she became so annoyed that she postponed the writing of the composition. Everybody then prepared for the first theme. I even put in a lot of effort and time. On Monday she assigned the second theme only. She remained adamant to our pleadings. Even I implored her in vain. The second theme was quite out of my line, though to be honest, I must admit that I could have done all right if I had wanted to. But I didn't in the least want to, and I made no effort. When she saw that I was not writing at all, she shook her wise head right at me, so that I finally wrote three little sentences. Then I went back to doing nothing. Angrily and abruptly she told the class to hand in the compositions since some of us were just wasting time. During the lesson she treated me very coldly. I did have a bad conscience. At 11 o'clock I went to her to ask her what extra work I should do. She coolly told me and then said: "Tell me, Kaya, why didn't you write?" As I was silent, she continued: "Honestly now, you just didn't feel like it." I admitted this, and explained to her my annoyance at the useless studying of the other theme. Then she said laughing: "But unfortunately one can't always do what one likes, and to get to the heart of the matter, I will tell you what I think. You were being obstinate!" With that she went off and left me standing there deeply hurt by this expression, which one really uses only when speaking to children, but also depressed and

[29]

sad that "she" was cross with me. All the following week she was cool toward me, as never before, so that I was getting quite desperate. But this morning she was so sweet to me that I am perfectly happy. She asked me, among other things, whether we crib from each other in class when doing our French homework, to which I replied that we only did a little comparing. Our friendship is repaired again.

20 February 1901

Why? Why is everything beautiful on earth given to me, only not the highest thing, not love! I have a heart so needing love, the words apply to me too:

> To love and be loved
> is the highest bliss on earth.*

Only the first is granted me. Yes, I love Mother, Berndt, Herr Schulze, Frl. Banning, etc., with all my heart. But who loves me??

27 February 1901

Last time I wrote I was certainly in a very melancholy mood. Today almost the opposite. It was heavenly in school today too. School gets finer every day, and more divine, alas, when I think that I can only enjoy it for 3½ weeks

---

* A typical verse used in "poetry albums." [Ed.]

more. (Boo-hoo!!) I have a lot to do today: 1. copy my whole composition, 2. declamation evening at school from 6 to 7, declamation at the Singer family's from 8:30 to 10.

7 March 1901

The evening was fine, there was splendid declaiming. It really is a pleasure. My talent for this almost excuses me for my total lack of understanding for music. —In school it's nice. Today I got back my composition, with which I hadn't taken much trouble. For I scribbled it down in an hour on the first day (8 pages), then didn't look at it for 2 weeks, and on the last day rattled it off in 2 hours. For this poor product I got an "A." Unbelievable. Yesterday Berndt did his Arbitur. Great celebration in the evening. Almost all our friends were on hand. Twenty-four in all. "He" came too, said he would have to leave in ¼ of an hour, but stayed 5 hours like the others. I talked a lot of nonsense when I spoke with him yesterday, for we had been looking at our marks in the school record, which of course is forbidden. He said to me: "Last time you had only 'A—' for arithmetic in your record." I: "This time I have a full 'A.' " Suddenly I got a terrible scare and said: "Oh my, I am not supposed to know this." He laughed: "How *do* you know it?" I went dark red and silent. He: "Do you already know all your marks?" I, impertinent again: "So far as they have been written down." We danced afterward, everybody had a good time.

8 March 1901

Today Mother went to a card-reading fortuneteller. It is really fabulous what she knows. She told Mother: "You have two children, the 19-year-old is probably a son?" Mother: "Indeed he is." She: "He won't be home for the next 5 years. (Berndt is going into military service and then to study.) Your daughter is 15. Her only passion is for books and study. And she will get far. Between 17 and 18 she will have some battles because the question of getting engaged will come up for her. But this will pass because she has set a very high aim for herself in her studies. This aim she will achieve. She will take a much respected, special place in the world and will belong to a very fine circle. You," she said, turning to Mother, "you will be mostly with your daughter later on. You will reach 75. You have been through so many difficulties in the last 7 to 10 years that you could write a book about it. A relative on your husband's side (Astrid) has caused you much sorrow and will bring you much more. You husband has business in a foreign country. Just now a change is going on in his business. He is here now, will be going away in June. He is a hot-tempered, nagging character, but not bad. Up to now he has had no great misfortune. This ship will founder on a rock. You husband will not reach 68, he will die in the next 3½ years, through a stroke and an accident in the country. Ten months after his death you will receive a proposal of marriage. And a brilliant position will be offered to you. In August of this year you will have the opportunity to make a fine long voyage. You are moving now, the house you are moving into is surrounded by trees. In the next three years you will be having a lot of trouble with your nerves and abdominal region."

9 March 1901

Religion Lesson

Today we had a splendid religion lesson again. Herr Schulze is not totally liberal (liberal in the bad sense), but so nicely in the middle between orthodox and liberal, inclining somewhat more to the latter. I will try to give an idea of how the lesson went. We were involved in an explanation of the concept of the 3rd Article, and I brought up the question: "What sort of difference is there really between confessing, 'I believe in God,' and confessing, 'I believe in the Holy Ghost'?"

He: "That would bring us back to our old question concerning the Trinity." This I had to admit. He: "This is a problem that can probably never be solved to our satisfaction. Even in early Christian times it was very much argued about. One can imagine: God, the original creative power; Jesus, divinity manifest, bringing salvation; the Holy Ghost, guardian, reigning in the heart. But they are just as much one as the *various* powers in a person are one, as: willing, feeling, perceiving, etc."

Afterward we talked again about Christ's personality, mostly in an exchange between him and me. He also said that there was a divine spark in every human being. It was in Christ that God manifested himself most. In such a way that he should be an ideal human being in the truest sense of the word. —Well, it was heavenly, and he was heavenly. It's so touching, how he responds to all my questions. He is my inner God. I am afraid that when I no longer have him as a teacher, I may go astray. In any case I shall be *very* grateful to him for what he was, is, and, I hope, still will be to me.

15 March 1901

Frl. Banning

Today is "her" birthday, the birthday of Frl. Banning. Happy day, on which she saw the light of the world, etc. I don't want to indulge in sentimentalities. Well, I carved for her a frame for a photograph and brought it to her this morning. I got to her house at 7 minutes to 8, and the maid announced me. At last I was led into her very prettily arranged room.

I: Good morning, Frl. Banning. Hearty congratulations.

SHE: Good morning. How kind of you to come.

    (She gives me a kiss! I give her the carved frame.)

I: Please forgive me for this invasion so early in the morning.

SHE: Unfortunately I can't ask you to stay, for I haven't had my coffee yet.

    (She opens the packet and thanks me for it.)

    But your photograph belongs in here. Am I not getting that?

I: (Stammered something.)

SHE: Promise me. But keep the promise too. You only have one more week at school. But you'll come and see me at school or here won't you?

I: Most gladly.

I don't remember what more we said. I'm afraid I have adored her terribly. Anyway I was blissful as I trundled home. I burst into tears on my way for joy and sorrow that I shall be losing her soon now.

18 March 1901

Reading

Among the numerous books I have got hold of there are only a few that keep me fascinated for any length of time. You automatically get more to read than is good for you. But I think I can say that the novels I have read haven't done me any harm. Some of course fascinated me for the moment—the next day I didn't think about them any more. Of this kind of book (I'll call them *Schmöker**) my favorites are the Karl May travel novels. After having read, thought (probably very little?), and heard a lot that's clever, those are really the nicest sort of thing one can read—even when one is tired out. 1. They are not love stories, 2. they are not so awfully stupid, 3. they are *very exciting*, 4. they are nicely stimulating and humorously written—whether everything happened the way he writes it, I don't care. But these books too are, as I have said, *Schmöker*—they cannot give true, deep, enjoyment. Books that do give it can carry me away enraptured; I read them once, twice, after a short time again—and again. Such books are:

FELIX DAHN: *The Battle for Rome, Julian the Apostate,* and *Odin's Consolation.*
SCHEFFEL: *Eckehart*

The Battle for Rome: If I were a poet, *mon Dieu*, then I would know what my work would be—and yet I'd be a long time choosing who my hero should be, Teja, Wittiches, or Totila? I don't know whom I like best.

I think Teja is the grandest. I've learned all his songs by heart. Cethegus too has aroused my admiration. Julian— I'm always furious when people speak contemptuously about him. His personality has always interested me, and now since I have read Dahn's book, I'm all aflame with

---

* Entertaining light novels or stories. [Ed.]

enthusiasm about him. He has become my 3rd historical enthusiasm. I have set him beside Brutus and Napoleon.

Odin's Consolation: Only a totally shriveled, hardened heart could be left cold by these old Germanic deities. It may sound awfully unchristian, but if I had been an ancient German I would not have renounced my faith.

Reinbeck, 3 April 1901

Difficult and Eventful Days

I haven't written for a long time. I had often taken pen in hand to pour out my heart to you, my dear diary, but I never found quiet and time enough. Now at last! I hardly know where to begin. Well, I'll try putting it in chronological order; like this:

19 March, Tuesday

Mother and Berndt had both gone out. The master of the house and I were alone at home, he in the front, I in the back. All of a sudden he enters my room, stands before me and says: "Mother is unaccountable." Of course I was terribly shocked that he should dare to say this to me, who loves Mother above everything. I gave him a piece of my mind. Conversations of this sort always take the same turn. He: Mother makes us all unhappy. I: We are so unspeakably happy when you are not here. Mother is our greatest happiness, our one and all, etc. Such conversations excite me a good deal, though I really shouldn't get excited about them because something happens every day. You gradually become dulled to it.

21 March, Thursday

This morning I played truant. Which reminds me that I have forgotten to tell about another school episode. Satur-

day the 16th of March we had a physics lesson with Dr. Dietrich. He was fixing an iron plate for an experiment and laid it down all crooked. Hertha suddenly said: "It's crooked." Käthe: "It's quite crooked." I: "It's altogether crooked." He was furious and lectured us severely. Brrrr!! I.e., I couldn't help laughing. He was frightfully angry with me. I thought it was all over, but not on your life! Tuesday we peeked into the record of our marks, and there stood beside an "A" for my conduct, a "B" from Dr. Dietrich. This left me fairly cold. The last lesson was Dr. Dietrich's. So the gentleman began to give me a sermon on my lack of apology. He said he would give me a "C" for conduct. I already knew better because I had seen the "B." I did apologize after class, because I hoped he would give me an "A" after all, and in this I was not mistaken.*
—But now I had enough of this bad business, I didn't want any more lessons with him. By rights we were to have 4 more lessons with him: Thursday, the first, I didn't come till 10 o'clock; Saturday, the last—I didn't want to be missing on Saturday, so I put on such an act of feeling sick to Frl. Emmerich that she sent me home before the last lesson. Tuesday I didn't show up at all, and Thursday the first I was absent too.

Now follow indescribably difficult days provided for Mother and us by the master of the house and by Pastor R. I don't want to write about it, for pen and paper would rebel against writing down anything so coarse and mean, committed furthermore by Christians (even orthodox ones). But it is conceivable that I could only hate the Pastor. My day of confirmation was not a day of blessing for me. —On the contrary, it was a great piece of hypocrisy, for I professed belief in the teachings of Christ, the doctrine of love, with hatred in my heart (and for my nearest, at that). I

---

* Now I have made a mistake in dates, all this was a week earlier. So, now I'm back again at the 21st.

feel too weak to follow Christ. Yet I long for the faith, firm as a rock, that makes oneself *and others* happy. I hardly dare to love Christ, he who was love, the pure one, although he stands before me as a glorious ideal. I hardly dare to pray, for I don't want to be hypocritical. Until I feel strong enough to pray sincerely and to act accordingly, I would rather not pray at all. Only one thing can I plead for, like a cry from the deep: "Lord help me" or "give me understanding," but I am too listless to believe—there are so many things to think of. —It is evening now. I have already said goodnight to the gentleman downstairs, and will now just fill in the gap up to the present. It certainly is no pleasure to sit downstairs—with that man.

So now Tuesday: the 26th March was my confirmation day—very strenuous. The only nice thing was Herr Schulze. I think I shall always and always be fond of him, even if other crushes command my emotional energies. Herr Schulze is for me a point of rest in the confusion, in the restlessness of life, to which I cling in thought. From now on he is just my real friend, for as teacher I saw him last at the farewell party on the 23rd of March. The parting was very difficult. And yet I hardly felt it, because it seemed to me like a bad dream, not like reality. This winter there were too many impressions, happenings; besides which I came at once into different work and different circles and stimuli, so that I hardly had time to reflect about it all. The days following my confirmation were filled with visits. Friday I also went to see Frl. Banning, who had sent me this card,* which of course pleased me very much. Then I went to Herr Schulze. He was charming as always. When I thanked him afterward for everything he had given me in these last years, he said: "Don't mention it. It gave me such pleasure to work with you, and I learned a lot

---

* The card was in the diary. [Ed.]

in the process." In the evening he came to see us and brought me back my poetry album. He wrote something in it for me, playing on the idea that I must now be called "Karen." I was frightfully pleased with it. Thursday we had to hand over our dear boy, who is now in military service in Erlangen. We miss him very much. —Then came the move!! Truly, Kaya, you speak a great word calmly. It was dreadful. Now at last we are settled.

I suppose I should make a new chapter here for the new chapter in my life.

Now how can I describe the impression the first 3 days at the Gymnasium made on me?? General impression: overwhelming, bewildering. It is something totally different. So I should probably describe the separate impressions. All the teachers gave inaugural speeches, which struck me as awfully funny. Our mathematics teacher, Dr. Bohnert, is very nice, clear and comprehensible, amiable in explaining. The Latin one, Dr. Christensen, is so far just loathesome. He never asks me questions, since I sit way in the back. The German one, Dr. Ahlgrim, is very good-looking and, *last but not least* [in English], the history teacher, Dr. Ziebarth, seems to be nice and interesting. A lady, with whom we also have English and French, sits in on the lessons: Frau Grube. One thing I've already noticed, I'm only now beginning to learn what "learning" means.

Reinbeck, 21 April 1901

I like going to the Gymnasium, though except for history lessons it is pretty dry. Two girls have struck me especially: Gertrude Piza, who has already had a year at a Gymnasium in Hannover and has a clever, impressive face, and Alice H.,

also from the Convent School, because of her bright wit.
Evenings employ my best recreation: declamation. It's really
going divinely. My favorite poems are: "Hektor's Farewell"
(Schiller), "Salas Gomez" (Chamisso), "Death of Tiberius"
(Geibel), "The Power of Song" (Schiller), "Bertran de
Born" (Uhland), and countless others that don't occur to
me just now. I went to see Frl. Banning and Herr Schulze
on Wednesday. Both charming—*of course* [in English]. I
took pussy willows to Frl. Banning and my picture. She
promised me that she would visit us here sometime. Will
she do it? Spring is coming on full force in Reinbeck, and I
delight in every bud and little leaf that comes out. Our
garden is being prepared now too. Oh, if I could always
live like this, in and with Nature, it strengthens body and
mind; one becomes good here. (If only my Father were
gone.)

28 April 1901

Today the Sternbergs, friends of the master of the house
from America, were here. Friday Pastor V.R. invited me to
the Wallenstein Trilogy. I was enormously pleased, but had
to decline on account of the Sternbergs, one of those
sacrifices one makes with a heavy heart and yet so easily.
I enjoy school very much. We have to cram hard. I like
the history teacher Dr. Ziebarth best. He is interesting, his
classes less so.

2 May 1901

I've been at the Gymnasium for 3 weeks now, and am already beginning to enjoy it enormously. Latin and mathematics are, of course, rather dry, but I like both these subjects, especially the latter, quite well. Arithmetic is rather difficult for me as usual. The other lessons are better, and I always look forward to them. In German we are doing grammar, usually the dullest subject for me, now enormously interesting; as it is a broader study of the German language. He continually asks me questions, which of course I like very much. My objective is still medicine. I think of it as by far the most interesting, although not the most pleasant, study—if my powers hold out (pecuniary, mental, and physical).

15 May 1901

Six weeks at the Gymnasium. I feel perfectly at home and enjoy it immensely, only when I see Herr Schulze or Frl. Banning longing grabs me with all its claws. He was here all day Sunday. We made a trip to Aumühle. In the evening I was in a sentimental melancholic mood. Yes, the years at the Convent School were glorious—at least I still have the beautiful memories of those *tempi passati*. I shall soon be going again to see my friends in the Convent School, where I am always received with joy. Saturday is Whitsun, his birthday—I'll go to see her and him. Today I wrote an extemporary Latin composition. There is as yet little to say about my schoolmates. One, Lisa B., is an interesting *Backfisch* type. Gets crushes on many people like mad, is pretty and rich, but a little superficial, I think.

Another, Gertrude P., I like very much. Conditions at home look sad. The master of the house informed us today that his ship would probably not be ready before Christmas. Delightful prospect. Well, at least I haven't gone to church with him again since Communion. I shall probably go some time later when he is gone. But as it is . . . I cannot listen to his sensuous, materialistic, illogical, intolerant views of everything high and holy. He is simply a low, ordinary, stupid character, who cannot rise to higher things. If he would at least put orthodox theory into practice. He is so egotistic, so without self-discipline and self-respect, gentleness, and what are called the virtues of a Christian . . . like the worst heathen. —No! Either/or: Either be no Christian, or a Christian who can deny himself and take his cross upon himself, who has the *firm will* to become a child of God with the Lord's help. But in any case not talk so much about it, not be a Christian with your mouth and your sentiments and no Christian in your actions.

27 May 1901

Whitsun is no real festival of joy for us this time. Berndt away—and the master of the house here—and today, to top it all, my step-brother Enoch is coming, a sandy-haired, fundamentally bad person, the sight of whom makes Mother and me quite sick.

Poor little Mutti;* this too. How the fellow can even dare to come into her house again. —But I aways say, the whole pack has no sense of honor at all. We are having a week's vacation now. Saturday I paid Herr Schulze a birthday visit. He was horribly boring. Frl. Banning was not at home. Oh, my dear diary, I can hardly admit to you what a weakling I am. Out of sight, out of mind; no sooner am

* "Mommy" in German. [Ed.]

I in other surroundings than I begin to get ecstatic again. The last verse of a song automatically comes to mind:

Oh, would it but stay so forever.

It will not stay so, the sun will kiss
Us in its wandering down.
Ere it's gone, so large—and still—
You long will have loved another.

I did not think that I would begin again so soon with my enthusiasms.

19 June 1901

I don't understand myself, am dissatisfied with myself and everybody else. In the condition I am in now, I am absolutely good for nothing. I can only work hard 1 to 2 days a week, and for that I am mortally weak the next day. I constantly have the feeling that I'm going to collapse. Does it come from my longing for "her and him"?? From the irritating and so fatiguing daily excitements with Father here?? From sympathy with Mutti?? Because I see Mother suffering, or from my own occupations, in which I am perhaps not yet quite at home? *Je ne sais pas*, for I have not overworked myself *as yet* [in English]. If only I could work the way I would so much like to. Perhaps it's only a weakness of will that makes me succumb so often to my headache, limpness, lack of courage and desire? No, that shall not be: I *will* now be stronger than this other complaining me: I will.

16 August 1901

Summer vacation is over. Thank God. Such silliness. Beforehand good grades, everyone said I had the best. Well, one's first record in the Gymnasium is always rather amusing. An "A" only in history. But the best of this business was what I grossed in the process: 3 marks for the grades, 3 marks for a hat that only cost me 2, leaves 4 marks with which I bought myself a perfectly great book.

But now, my dear diary, I must widen your circle of acquaintances a little, namely to include the Holmberg family. I first met Tuti H., who is 9 months older than I, while on vacation in the dunes, where we made friends. A few years passed, a year and a half, I think, before we saw each other again. Then I went to the Convent School and we became close friends, both had crushes on Frl. Schöne, Herr Schulze, Karl May and even swore blood brotherhood à la Karl May, i.e., we very carefully slit a finger till a microscopically small drop came out, diluted it with water, and drank, brrrr . . . oh dear, when one is still young. And all of a sudden, bang! the whole glory was over. The way I write this makes it almost sound as if the whole affair had left me cold. But that was not so. This loss hurt me deeply. I saw her seldom after that, for she left school a year ahead of me, and when we did meet we were distinctly polite, even friendly to each other. But each time it felt as though a sore spot had been touched. Well, we were in the "Kupfermühle" having lunch recently when the Holmberg family came in. (By the way, I like her father and one of her sisters quite well, but the mother hardly counts among my crushes.) So, and then—we walked alone a little and found that we had been frightfully stupid before; it wasn't exactly a great reconciliation party, but something of the sort, well, anyway she'll be coming to see me soon.

In school we are carrying on. In English class for instance, I did nothing today but read the *die Berliner Range,** consumed pears, plums, chocolate, and candy. Lisa B. is the most mischievous. Frau Grube told her today that she would see to it that Lisa is excused from English and French. Mostly I am with Alice H. We are both crazy about Frl. Banning, who has invited us to coffee next Friday.

22 August 1901

Tomorrow we go to Frl. Banning. Of course, we are both awfully glad, but we try to persuade ourselves that it is all the same to us or even a bother. On that account I've just been on the Heideberg alone, for Mutti† is awfully down again, and picked some flowers for her. Oh, it was so lovely up there, the beautiful landscape spread in a sweep at my feet. I love such a wide view because it brings peace to my heart, which, though only in its *Backfisch* state, still is often quite sad and discouraged. For things are bad at home, and Mutti, my all, is so ill and unhappy. Oh, how I would love to help her and cheer her up. If only she had, as I do, some sort of school or other means of distraction. Even though I often leave in the morning with tears in my eyes, I always come back cheerful. But after all, it really is very nice at school.

---

* Literally "The Berlin Lassie" (or naughty girl). [Ed.]
† "Mommy" in German. [Ed.]

7 September 1901

I would almost like to say with Lenau, "I bear a deep wound in my heart." The affair isn't quite so tragic after all, but still so similar. To you, my dear diary, I will confide it. To you alone. You're probably preparing yourself for a love story?? No, nothing of that sort. You know, I recently saw my formerly dearly beloved friend Tuti H. again and invited her to come and see us. I looked forward to her visit very much, attaching to it the high hopes of having a friend again since I had been totally without one for a year. Somebody should have called out to me, "Shout not for joy, for the powers of Fate are jealous. Premature rejoicing infringes on their rights."

I am disappointed—be it that she has changed, or I. The bit of green color in my heart has turned into an indifferent grey, and I am lonelier than before. For neither Alice nor Tuti can give me what I expect from a girl-friend, at least not up to now. But I won't grumble about it. It may yet work out. In the winter I may be able to find boy-friends again, perhaps in dancing class, with which I am supposed to be plagued this winter. —One thing more, my dear diary (I'm going to call you "Kitten"), I must tell you and still don't want to, for what will you think of my fickleness? After Easter I firmly resolved to go in for no more enthusiasms, and since then I've already done so a number of times—1. for Frl. Banning, 2. for Dr. Ahlgrim, 3. for Dr. Ziebarth, who has just come back from his trip. He is divine, you are laughing Kitten? Yes, I confess it honestly—I am a stupid *Backfisch* with my eternal crushes.

22 December 1901

So Kitten, day after tomorrow you will be a year old. A ripe old age if one thinks of all you have experienced and lived through with me. Christmas is on the threshhold. Holidays are here again. For the first time I have been looking forward to them with real joy, for I felt and still feel quite enervated. It was a little much, and I am not of the strongest. Well, I do have the best marks. But that doesn't affect me, for I myself feel that I am frightfully stupid, and that is a rather depressing experience. You know, I have always been told that I was clever, and I had eventually come to believe it although I was never quite convinced of it. You consolingly remind me of Socrates. Alas Kitten, his experience was different from mine. I live altogether for school. Mornings in school and afternoons at home cramming for school. But it gives me joy, inexpressible joy. My favorite subject now is mathematics. And accordingly I have a crush on Dr. Bohnert? No, Kitten, you've miscalculated this time. I do like him very much, but a crush?? No, that's something else. You ask about Scipio? Alas, just think, he is gone since Michaelmas (September 29th). Brrrr, that was a shock when he told us he could no longer teach us. When he was gone his place was taken by Lorenz, called Don Carlos, a handsome young man of 28. At first I was crazy about him. But he is so impudent and unfair, and I didn't want to go on wasting my love on him. And just think, I have now entered into a state that you will hardly understand. I haven't a crush on anybody. That would be miraculous? —But it's true. Perhaps it comes from the beneficent influence of mathematics or maybe I'm already so old and sensible? For I am already 16. The girls at the Gymnasium have founded a newspaper, "A Virginal Organ for Supervirgins." That sounds to me rather "*mad*" [in English], but we aren't so at all. On the contrary!! A nice atmosphere prevails there. I've gotten more intimate with Alice.

A good happy holiday, my Kitten.

2 February 1902

Heavy clouds are obstructing the clear sky. Alice, my dear Alice, that child of Nature, who has indeed grown strange through a love-starved youth and wrong upbringing, has been, if not exactly thrown out, nevertheless forced to leave at Easter on account of bad behavior. And what bad behavior? Well, yes, she was unruly before Christmas. Since then she has pulled herself together very much. A triviality—an innocent remark during class—these super-clever pedagogues made into a big affair. That means they expect a person to change completely in a few days on command. Oh, cruel tyrants!! How I hate them! How could I ever have had a crush on a teacher. —But no, they aren't all like that. And "she," Frl. Banning, belongs to the few exceptions. But then who doesn't tyrannize? Only trees are allowed to grow free to the sky—but they too are pruned.

4 March 1902

A delegation went off to the honorable gentleman to plead for Alice. He asked for another two weeks to think it over. They are to go to him on Sunday and learn his decision.

I have been absent for two weeks. Otherwise I might have been frantic about it, now it's all the same to me. Till Easter I'm not allowed to do any homework.

All the better [in English]: Then I'll be able to work for "him." Oh yes, Kitten doesn't even know who "he" is. Well, he is Herr Ernst Schrumpf, an actor at the Court

Theater, where he is unfortunately not properly appreci-
ated. He is a Thuringian and since last autumn was court
actor in Stuttgart, attracted enthusiastic admirers there
(naturally), but had to leave because of intrigues. He is
married to a very nice lady, and has a lovely big dog with
which he always goes walking now. He is handsome, big,
very bright. And from this "he" I'm to get—just guess—
no, it's too beautiful! You can't guess?? Lessons in declamation. I'm swimming in bliss. Tomorrow is the first.

6 June 1902

New era of world history. Very anxious to know what's
next. Now, I want to keep you on tenterhooks a bit longer
and first give you a review of the last 3 months, since I am
guilty of not having told you anything yet. Not that
nothing happened . . . *au contraire*. So far school had
occupied my mind completely. I was even able to put my
fondness for declamation at its service. That has changed.
In the Gymnasium I couldn't make any use of my talent
for reciting at all. No wonder that it became an independent
rival alongside school. First school was preponderant, then
with declamation lessons a threatening equilibrium appeared. And now school can hardly dare present itself as a
competitor without making itself ridiculous. Why, in a
year and a quarter it will have vanished totally from the
earth, and I will be living for art and art alone. I'm going
on the stage!! Not tomorrow, not even the day after tomorrow, but as I said, in a year and a quarter, because
Mutti won't let her chick out from under her wings. I
shall perhaps still take my teacher's examination with Frl.
K., where it is supposed to be very easy. I shall go there
today to inform myself about everything. Around 1902,
when I have become 18, I am to go wherever he is, to be

prepared by him for my profession; I hope to Berlin, for he is going there now. Oh dear, Kitten, I see your indignant countenance.

"You're telling me all sorts of plans, and I don't understand anything about it. How have you arrived at this? It's a pretty big step, after all, from a fondness for declamation to going on the stage! And anyway, are you allowed to do it."

I am deeply contrite. Yes, you are right, I forget what lies bright as the sun before my childish gaze is still a castle in Spain to you. . . . Well, my talent is greater than I thought, and since I always had the most ardent wish to go to the theater, it has now expressed itself with doubled strength. The longing was nourished by the glorious declamation lessons with Herr Schrumpf, though we talked only a little about it. Mother feels totally opposed to it. I had not yet come out quite openly with my wish. Then on Sunday, June 1st, I was alone with him at a coffee party where I was to recite something. So we came, I don't know how, to speak about my going on the stage. We talked a long time about it, and he promised he would speak to Mutti on my behalf. Then and there it became quite clear to me that this was the right road for my life; I was determined to take up the battle with all inimical powers and was certain that, with courage born in despair over my life's happiness and with great confidence in my good cause, I would come through victorious. Blow on blow. Monday a pleading letter to Berndt to bring Mother around, and a frank hint to Mother. Tuesday bombarded Mutti with two poems in which I besought her to let me go. Unfortunate excitement and headache for Mutti, for which I was frightfully sorry because she really has enough other trouble already, so I didn't need to make any more for her. But my happiness—oh, momentous word, only in these days have I come to know you and your blessed influence—was at stake. I could not do otherwise. Early Thursday morning Mother, very excited, suddenly went off to Hamburg, no one knew where. The morning was frightful. She came back at last and now hear, Kitten, if you don't know it already, what mother-love is. Her favorite plan was to see me graduate and be a scholar. She doesn't like stage life. She would have to give up her child earlier. And now love for her child has triumphed in her heart; she will allow it. In any case, after a year and a quarter. So, first digest this, Kitten, then I will tell you more.

Third Diary

1903–1904

Begun Winter 1903, at 17

Vidi, audivi, legi, feci

—KAREN HAMBURGENSIS

SONNI

www

Times of Transition

Everything in me is storming and surging and pressing for light that will resolve this confusion. I seem to myself like a skipper who leaps from his safe ship into the sea, who clings to a timber and lets himself be driven by the sea's tumult, now here, now there. He doesn't know where he is going.

Homeless am I.
With no sheltering abode I rove about.
Safe and quiet
I lived in the old masonry
stronghold that thousands of years
had built for me.
It was gloomy and close—
I longed for freedom.
A little light only, a little life.
Quietly, driven by an inner urge,
I began to dig.
Bloody my nails, weary my hands.
Mockery from others and bitter scorn
the end reward for the endless toiling.
The stone came loose—
one more powerful grip and

it fell at my feet.
A ray of light pressed through the opening
greeting me kindly,
inviting and warning,
waked a shiver of delight in my breast.
But hardly had I drawn into myself
this first shimmer
when the rotting masonry broke to pieces
and buried me in its fall.
Long I lay
thinking nothing
feeling nothing.
Then my strength stirred, so freshly drunk-in,
and I lifted the fragments with muscular arm.
All aglow with strength,
bloom of the storm,
delight flowing through me
I looked out far and wide.
I saw the world,
I breathed life.
The brightness of light
almost blinded me—
yet soon I was used to its brilliance.
I looked about.
The view was almost too wide,
my sight could roam to unlimited distances.
Oppressive almost
the New, the Beautiful invaded me.
At that an all-powerful longing seized me,
almost bursting my breast,
and it drove me forth to wander
in order to see, to enjoy
and to know the All.
And I wandered—
restlessly driven
I rove about,

released from the dungeon
I joyfully sing in jubilant tones
the old song to life,
to freedom, to light.
Only an anxious question often hems me in:
toward what goal am I striving?
A gentle longing, a mild lament:
When at last will you come to rest?
And I think I understand the answer
in the murmuring of the woods:
"Rest is only behind the prison walls,
life, however, does not know it."
Watchful searching
with no cowardly complaints,
restless striving
with no weary despair:
that is life—
dare to endure it.

February 1903

I Myself   17 years old

I really should not read anything—I mean no books,
but only myself. For only one half of my being lives, the
other observes, criticizes, is given to irony.

I have made a clumsy attempt to describe my mood in
this crazy poem. I can describe it better with a single
word: chaos. There is such disordered turmoil in me, that
I myself cannot burrow my way through this labyrinth.
And yet: I am beginning to burrow. I often think I already
see the light toward which I am struggling. Then again I
get deeper and deeper into the chaos.

In the winter before my confirmation I made my last attempt to pray. And I remember how only the same 4 words passed my lips: "Lord, give me truth."

Now I know that no one can give that to me, but only through my own work will I get a clear view, or perhaps not get it.

I asked this morning whether I might join a class in animal dissection, and I was turned down with a miserable "Don't bother me again with that." So probably nothing will come of animal dissection. *Et voila* a substitute: I shall take myself to pieces. That will probably be more difficult, but also more interesting. What shall I begin with?

This summer I thought a great deal and read a great deal. In consequence I have developed with uncanny rapidity from an intellectual and moral point of view.

The most interesting question for me is that of morality, for I think that it is more important for practical living than the question of intelligence. That is why I want to talk about it here first. I very vividly remember one particular day. It was a Monday in February 1903, the month that I spent in Hamburg. Alice and I were walking together after school. We started talking about the sudden death of Dr. K., our zoology teacher whom we liked so much, and about whom we had just heard that Monday. Then our conversation, as it does with 17-year-olds, turned to questions about love. I told Alice, with an indignant expression, that a few days before "an impudent gentleman" had followed me. Alice grinned at my indignation and said: "*Sancta simplicitas*, what's wrong with that? Did you go with him?" I looked at her: "Would you do such a thing? Go with a strange gentleman?"

Alice: "That all depends on how they look. If they look decent and nice, why not?"

I: "Don't tell me you meet them half-way?"

Alice: "Hm, not exactly, but if it's something special one walks a little slower, or looks in a shop window or something of that sort. By the way, I'd like to tell you something else. It just occurred to me. Well, last evening, L. and I went out for some fun. Suddenly an awful downpour. In desperation we waited under one umbrella for a streetcar. Of course the wretched thing didn't come. Suddenly a gentleman came rushing toward us, very handsome, very elegant, about 40, and said we'd better come into the café with him for a little while until the rain stopped. We were just feeling very enterprising and jovial: so into the place we went. We consumed various little cakes and had a great time. His name is B., he said—he's a writer and was *tout à fait* smitten with L. He said we were the only sensible girls in the whole of Hamburg. Oh, you know, one joke after another. At first quite innocent. Then he asked me what I thought about love between women, just think how shocking."

I: "Well, what's wrong with that? It certainly isn't anything horrible if we two love each other?"

Alice: "You idiot, of course not. *That* is when they are perverted." (She followed with a long explanation of perversion and then she went on.)

Alice: "I think L. likes him too. They want to meet again this evening. I think I'd better go along, or L. may do something silly. I'm not quite sure of her."

I said I certainly didn't find it especially nice, if she went with a strange gentleman, but that I didn't know what particular silly things she might do.

Alice: "Now little Karen, don't pretend to be so stupid. If L. goes to his room with him and he asks her, then she will do it, and that of course would be frightful."

I stood there dumbfounded: "No, Alice, it isn't possible. Do you really know these things? I believe I've misunderstood you. You mean L. would do the worst thing a girl can do?"

Alice: "Why not? It comes awfully easy. I almost did it myself once." She followed with a description of an attempt at seduction.

[59]

I, finally after a silence: "But if L. were to get a baby. . . ."

Alice: "Oh, she won't be that stupid. Actually I don't believe that she'll do it."

I: "I thought such things didn't happen at all in our circles."

Alice, laughs: "In masses. A girl in our class did it—and even with her father."

I was speechless with horror. Alice told me the details and told me who it was.

We went to see Frau Doree. Alice wanted to bring her flowers. Then Alice said: "She used to be crazy too. Had one after the other. But what does it matter? In W.'s theater group there was a girl who had one every evening. The others were even indignant about it. So W. said: 'What do you want, children, after all she doesn't sell herself.'" Then I was informed about those creatures who sell themselves for a little money. It was my first glimpse into that miserable business, prostitution.

Our ways then parted. I felt very exhausted. The whole dreadful knowledge all at once. It was too much. And then I couldn't even be left quietly to myself and let the storm within subside. Tante Emma, Frl. Stental, and I were invited to old Tante Clara's and had to chatter about something or other the whole afternoon. Tante Emma surely noticed that I was not my usual self. I blamed everything on the impression Dr. K.'s death had made on me. They understood my "grief" and praised me for my alleged gratitude to my teacher. In reality I wasn't thinking about it. I had for the first time—no, not for the first time, for I had already had a dark suspicion what that business with the "stork" was all about—bitten into the apple of knowledge. It was very sour. I had to digest it first.

From there on I began to investigate. I was able to extract a lot from my engaged friend, Tuti, the "initiated," and through her learned about the things which. . . . Soon after that I heard that L. had "fallen" and was B.'s lover.

Alice accompanied this information with the words: "I say, it's horrible, but I now feel that there's nothing wrong with it." Upon which little Karen, naturally, burst into excited moral sermons: "How *can* you, Alice, it really is the worst thing one can do." Alice meaningfully shrugged her shoulders.

What happened to me then probably happens to everybody. I avidly picked up everything that could reveal to me something on these sensitive points. I had a preference for walking in the streets of the prostitutes. I read a book about "Prostitution in Paris." I read Zola's *Nana*. I often read Maupassant novels which L. brought along to school. I read poems of Marie-Madeleine "On Cyprus." And though I resisted, though tortured by pricks of conscience, I began to get enthusiastic about these poems. They stirred sensual pleasure in me for the first time. I read Bilche's *Love Life in Nature*, I read Wolff's *Tannhäuser*—and I finally got so far as to doubt my statement about the only sin a woman can commit. One question occupied my mind for weeks, even months: is it wrong to give oneself to a man outside of marriage or not? I answered now in the affirmative, now in the negative.

Only very gradually did I become certain that it is never immoral to give oneself to a man one really loves, if one is prepared to also bear all the consequences. How did I arrive at this joyously triumphant certainty? I don't know. I think a lot of things worked together. In the first place it was Shakespeare who helped me on the right track: "For there is nothing either good or bad but thinking makes it so."

One should base every consideration of things human on this sentence. A girl who gives herself to a man in free love stands morally way above the woman who, for pecuniary reasons or out of a desire for a home, marries a man she does not love. Marriage is something only external. It is bad—not theoretically—but when one comes to know how few marriages are really good ones. I know two families from our large circle of acquaintances of whom I guess this is the case. But the one couple are pretty limited people, the other very superficial. The other marriages?? What a mess!

All our morals and morality are either "nonsense" or immoral.

Will it ever change? And how? And when?

The dawn of a new time is breaking. I hope with all the strength of my young hope. Perhaps even the next generation will not know these battles, perhaps it will already be stronger than we are because more of them stem from a union of love. Perhaps more of the next generation will become mothers, true mothers, whose children are children of love. For how difficult it is today for a young girl to admit that she is having a child. The immorality of abortion will cease in that time—which perhaps will never come.

Sympathy 1903

My head is on fire. I groan, weep with despair and pain. I will look happy when someone comes into the room. Only no sympathy. Sympathy hurts, humilitates me. But if I show my suffering, it calls forth sympathy. So nobody is to know when I am suffering.

I lay my finger on my lips
and say: be silent, silent, silent.
For what can strangers be to you
that your inner self be shown them?

What do they feel of your suffering?
What do they know of your delight?

[62]

You may entrust yourself to heaven,
to the moon, the stars, the sun.

And to the clouds and the waves
and every flower, every twig,
but when you step once more among people
then think of me, and be silent, silent.

The same feeling humiliates or strengthens me. Only a
real friend will be able and be permitted to suffer with me.
How strengthening such sympathy is,
But how rare.
The *Poems of Marie-Madeleine* can at times intoxicate
me through their fire, through the glowing sensuality and
passion they breathe out. I believe passion is always con-
vincing. There are moments when I can feel with her the
intoxication of the senses, while often too I turn from it
with aversion. (Those must be the Philistine hours, or
perhaps the hours in which the intellect preponderates.)
These two natures, the intellectual and the sensual, are
battling in me. One's senses exult at her poems in unbridled
delight. One's intellectual nature turns away in disdain.
There is a daemonic magic in the poems. One cannot remain indifferent about them. One must take sides.

In part great perfection of form, ingratiating language
and style. In almost every poem she speaks of "boundless
deep desire." That is the underlying theme.

I believe that a *spiritualized great sensuality* is a sign of
a great personality, or can be. Limited people will show
themselves to be limited in sensuality too. Other great
personalities will feel a great desire of the senses and will
combat it because they think it is wrong. If they manage
that, it is certainly one of the greatest victories within a
person. But is the battle against these natural instincts and
desires right at all? I think of the Greeks, of the Dionysian
festivals with their most riotous sensuous exuberance! I

think of the Grecian Mysteries; I think of what a people the Greeks were, and I say: no, no, and again no. You ascetics, you petty bourgeois: is it perhaps envy of the have-not clan that makes you carry on this battle against sensual enjoyment?

Marie-Madeleine: The Three Nights

Beautiful, rapturously beautiful your poems, singer of love. But this book? Is it artificial? Is it overflowing fantasy? You are playing again on the one theme that you have mastered: desire, sensuality, the torments of love.

A book of fables that tells of those who are "crucified because they love."

By far the best is the "Second Night"—Maud, who is cold and a stranger to passionate feelings, envies the little Hindu girl who has found death in the brutal love-embrace of her betrothed.

The last sentences shook me to my inmost marrow through their truthfulness.

Do I feel guilty?

"All through the millennia there sounds always but the one cry: For love's sake. —And in the end, the very end, I will tell you the fable that is the most depraved of all."

The depraved fable, that is me. In my own imagination I am a strumpet! In my own imagination there is no spot on me that has not been kissed by a burning mouth. In my own imagination there is no depravity I have not tasted, to the dregs.

And in reality . . . !

But not even the tips of my fingers have been kissed. But there is nothing in the world more immaculate than I. I have committed mental sins, which are the worst because they destroy and do not create—because they are a sin against holy life!

Perhaps I am the saddest fable of them all.

[64]

The underlying idea of the book:

"When I think about love I always see a woman on a high throne. And round about her heaps of dead and wounded! Children's corpses and dead old men, men in their death throes and dying women, youths fighting their last battle and girls in their death agony!

"And all those dying eyes are prayerfully turned up to the woman on the high throne, the women with eyes deep as an abyss and a conqueror's smile.

"And the air is heavy with the groans of the dying and the torments are as the sea, endless, unbounded!

"But the woman smiles and smiles!"

Marie-Madeleine's poetry: Fantasy—often glowing with sacred fire—often frivolous. Always beautiful, gentle, dreamy—undefined longings, blurred—one-sided—always repeating—and yet beautiful, intoxicatingly beautiful.

Unsteady

I often used to have a dream—probably the consequence of a wild Indian story: the floor gave way—and my bed sank, and sank—slowly at first, then faster and faster. Always faster, always deeper my bed sank down—into the bottomless abyss.

I often have the same feeling now, but not in my sleep. Now it is reality. I lose the ground under my feet—desolate chaos surrounds me and enwraps me, more and more. Does every young person have to take such a plunge? Oh, dear Karen, delusions of grandeur again? You any more than the average? Strange, that it is so infinitely difficult for me to convince myself that I am something ordinary, an average person, one of the herd. *O Vanitas*!!

My ordinariness is already evident in my wanting very much—how pedantic—to know what I am in the religious, the moral sense: Christian, Deist, Pantheist, Monist, Atheist? Berndt declares that developing larvae like me describe themselves best as "Skeptics." Perhaps this enrichment is *assez bien*, for I consist of question marks, called into the world with pathos: I don't believe that! It is the mind that always negates.

I am anxious to know where I shall be washed ashore some day. Perhaps I'll become an orthodox Jew. *Qui lo sa?*

Then I might even end up getting a little thinner at the fasting cures on the Day of Atonement.

Hm, hm, how witty little Karen wants to be.

Does one have to believe anything at all? Obsolete!

One can know a whole lot, and for the rest one can at best say: to me the whole business is most plausible thus and so. It would be smartest of course to follow Berndt's recipe and not yield to any conjectures about final things. For one probably wouldn't get much further anyway. But I cannot deal with things from this glacier-like point of view. I have to analyze and explain everything in a nice clean-cut way—"I can't do otherwise." But it is terribly much.

I often wonder whether I'll make it.

Sins of Reading

If I ever had to bring up children, I would deprive them of one thing: books. Not all, of course. They could read all the classics, also *Faust*, but in unabridged editions, Indian books, history books, art history and history of civilization, biographies of great men (Frederick the Great, Napoleon, Goethe, Schiller). But no novels, no teen-age books, for instance.

Oh children, I wanted to put down my views about books and plays in this diary. If I only wrote down the titles here I would have more than enough to do.

So now just a selection of books and plays of the last 2 to 3 weeks:

VON HALBE: *Jugend, Strom* ["Youth," "Stream"]
HEBBEL: *Herodes und Mariamne* ["Herod and Mariamne"]

SCRIBE: *Glas Wasser* ["A Glass of Water"]
ANZENGRUBER: *Pfarrer v. Kirchfeld* ["The Pastor of Churchfield"]
KELLER: *Grüner Heinrich*
EBNER-ESCHENBACH: *Agave*
R. VOSS: *Rolla*
BURCKHARDT: *Griechische Kulturgeschichte* ["History of Greek Civilization"]
BÖLSCHE: *Liebesleven in der Natur, Bazillus-Affenmensch* ["Love Life in Nature," "Bazillus-Apeman"]
VISCHER: *Auch Einer* ["He Too"]
HECKEL: *Welträtsel* ["Enigmas of the World"]

And at that I have been limiting myself very much in my reading recently. How was it before? Frightful. So now I am making a fixed *reading plan* for myself: to begin with a lot about Greek civilization (Burckhardt, Goethe, Winkelman, Lessing).

DRAMA: *Jugend*, possibly also *Herodes und Mariamne*
NOVEL: *Auch Einer* by Vischer

And there's no more, Karen, do you hear?

31 December 1903

Awakened to Life

Till now eagerness, striving, anxious seeking for some inner hold—
Now divine rest.
Till now chasing after happiness in every form—now exultant happiness, heavenly joy in my heart.
Till now only half alive with the constant, reproachful question in my eyes of whether this is really living, this

everlasting monotony? —Now full, whole life, joy of life in my veins down to the littlest fingertip.

I thank you, old year, for having wakened me out of the twilight in your dying days.

I love you, dear year of 1903, because you have given me the highest and the best we human beings can have—love.

Don't meddle with the handiwork of your predecessor, 1904, but carry on her work.

The others have gone to the New Year's Eve sermon. I didn't want to be interrupted in my meditations by conventional last-day-of-the-old-year thoughts. On this evening one should officially let the old year pass before one's eyes once more. So, wind up the cinematograph. The show begins:

What, is the machine not in order? All figures and scenes are blurred and in dizzying speed. The series of pictures must soon end. There, now comes light and rest. The pictures are clear:

A lighted Christmas tree—a small room—waltz music —2 who are dancing wildly.

Kunsthalle Art Museum—fire-worshipper—Mary Magdalen, two standing before it absorbed.

Alster—2 walking around.

Christmas room again—large open window toward the Alster, over the waves—2 dancing, dancing, dancing. Reinbeck woods—Woltorf Road—2 couples, the second always close behind the first. The first looking around impatiently—pine woods to the right—the first couple off to the side into the bushes—walking further and further—an open hill—a log across a little brook—

the camera snaps—

so, now it continues:

Reinbeck station and 2 waiting there—Berlin train comes in—

the camera snaps.
One train leaves—another comes.
A girl who gets in ———

New Year, I clink glasses with you!:
    To good friendship.

Hamburg, 11 January 1904

Waiting
    Why don't you write, Schorschi?
    Don't you know that my soul is sick with longing for a
        greeting from you?
    For a greeting your love sends me?
    For a word that you still love me.
    That it wasn't just a flirtation—our "happiness!"
    I wait, wait—wait from morning till evening.
    My first thought on waking, will a letter come from
        you today?
    And then waiting—waiting; at 9 and at 11,
    at 2 and at 4, at 6 and at 8, nothing for me.
    Oh, I know, I wrote you mockingly because you had
        excused
    yourself for a week-long silence.
    Can you not see deeper, deep down to the
        bottom of my soul that is hankering for a sign
        of your love, sparing as it may be?
    My love, my Baldur, my joy: do you no longer think
        of your little friend in Hamburg?
    Have you forgotten me, Schorschi?
        No sooner had my radiant eyes gazed into yours,
        No sooner had you pressed your first kiss upon
            my lips,
        When we had to say goodbye.

Do you love me still? Was it only a jest?
My heart quivers in a torment of doubt—
My eyes gaze dim into the distance.

Hamburg, 19 January 1904

"The battle in my heart has done raging." At first when
he had gone, I was as in a dream—then boisterous and
gay—then sentimental—then passionate and wild as the
ardently longed-for letter wouldn't and wouldn't come—
now quiet. Such a holiday mood.

Firm confidence that he loves me—perhaps also something of resignation—who can analyze one's own mood so
exactly? —Though I must often think that he, this charming person, cannot always, cannot much longer care for
me. What can I be to him? Must I now be satisfied with
those May days in December?

No, no it cannot last for long.

Happiness has no abiding-place
and the finest in springtime and love
is that sweet, that foolish word:
oh, would it but stay so forever.

And yet when I think that another girl—ah, intolerable.

But why then think of the future?
It is still the blossoming golden time
it is still the days of the roses—.

Reinbeck, 4 February 1904

What a strange condition one is in when one loves. It is a far greater chapter of one's life than those ordinarily designated as such, like confirmation, leaving school, losses by death. And I think it is a turn for the better. One becomes more self-conscious. And I believe that that in itself is an invaluable good, for the right sort of self-consciousness is definitely a basis for all independent development of character. One is in general freer, less dependent. For it is the first thing one really does on one's own initiative, on one's own responsibility. And another thing (to be meant as a joke), one becomes more concentrated. One's thoughts all gather around one focal point, around "him." Whether this is particularly favorable for one's thinking apparatus I have my doubts. For if "he is my thought day and night," how then should other thoughts have room?

No, I see I am composing a tract *à la* Ahlgrimm: What Effects has Love on the Development of Human Character?

A. good effects
B. bad effects

Oh, you Schorschi, if you were only here.

Yes, and sometime we will walk along "our" path and sit on the tree trunk across the little brook again and rest head on shoulder again and again and dare not speak in order not to disturb our happiness.

And if the sun is shining, then we will row together, we two,

you and I, I and you.
Yes, my dear, we'll be happy
and not think about what comes next, for all that
lies so far off still, so far—

It is still the blossoming, golden time.
Oh you beautiful world, how wide you are!
It is still the days of the roses.

The 24th of December seems so long to a child, so long.
It cannot wait for the bell to ring.
One hour creeps after another.
I am ill with longing and waiting and impatience.

25 February 1904

Clara Viebig

I can only marvel at the abundance and the riches revealed to me here.

We have books written with great art of profound observation, of loving absorption in the characters, but never
have I read one that doesn't grow ponderous in the process,
that doesn't forget the grace of motion because of the heavy
going.

By this mistake Frenssen, I think, comes to grief; he too
often gets heavy-footed.

Otherwise these two may well be compared. But Frenssen
sees only—or above all else—the amiable side of people.

Clara Viebig also sees the ugly side, she is the great
realist, she shows life as it is, in all its tragedy, in all its
pitiableness, but she doesn't break down under it.

There is one joy, one consolation for her, and that is
work, outward work and above all inward work.

I have seldom felt myself so much related to a character
in fiction as to this Nelda Dallmer in *Rheinlandstöchter*
["Daughters of the Rheinland"]. The one yearning cry for
a great love, this sensual exuberance that often seizes me
too and tumbles me about.

Shall I be able to work my way through to a greatness

and maturity like hers? What I have read so far of Clara Viebig's makes me anxious for more. In elegance a Maupassant, in depth and sound good health a Frenssen without his local limitations, and in observation and knowledge of the human, and above all the female, soul the equal of our greatest psychologists. In any case I shall never regret having read these books.

26 February 1904

Today, as I happened to open a book, I found the following passage:

> Always, you dearest, keep on impressing me—let me grow small, quite small alongside you—oh, be the strong man, the big man, the healthy man, the superior human being in whom I can lose myself completely, before whom I gladly and willingly kneel. Force me to my knees, dearest. For I am a woman. No good, shy little girl of the humble womanliness described in books— no, on the contrary. But just for this proud, free, independently thinking woman there is no sweeter lot than to be allowed to worship, to bow down in love.
>
> Oh, dearest—will you be my master?

Something for Lida Gustava Hymann!

11 March 1904

A week ago still exuberant and lively, bubbling with delight and love, and now weary, oh so weary—

My walk has grown heavy and dragging
and the sunny gleam in my eyes has disappeared.
I can still laugh, but I wonder about it myself,
when I hear it I am alarmed.
He was here for 4 days—
How jubilantly I had greeted him,
How I had longed for him the whole long winter through,
counted weeks, days, hours till he should come at last—
And then, then the dreadful knowledge came to me
that he has become indifferent to me, that he
does not love me any more.
I wept through the nights, and in the daytime
laughed with him and rejoiced in his springtime beauty.
And not a word of explanation on his part.
Was it to be taken for granted that he was cool and
    strange
to me whom once he had loved and kissed?
Then at the end a few cool sensible words
of good friendship, etc.
And soon he will have forgotten me.
Recently a morbid fear of death has often
seized me. I clung to life.
Now death does not seem to me so terrible any more.
Death, where is thy sting?
Has he any idea what torments and moves me?
I don't believe so.
And I was so sensible too, so sensible.
For I was as if paralyzed,
every warm word to him died on my tongue; for have I
any right to it without his love?

19 March 1904

I am now a senior, and I should be delighted.
I still cannot grasp it—2 days of brief happiness in love,
then all is gone.

I have to think of every tender word, of every kiss
he gave me then.
And now after 2 months, as though we had never
known each other.
Without a word of explaining—
and yet I love him so, I care so boundlessly
for him.
Now 10 days gone again and still
no word from him.
The others think I'm grieving because
you are away. Oh, how easy that would be to bear
if I knew that you loved me.
I dreamt about you, you were so loving then—
just no more dreaming, it is too hard
waking up.

Reinbeck, 23 March 1904

How gladly one lies to oneself, pretending the wished-for
has happened. So now I am imagining that it was only
reserve, which he owes to his 20 years, and that his inner-
most feeling for me is unchanged.

But this last breath of life of my young love's happiness
shows itself only hesitantly.

I don't believe it.

The first time, on the second day after his departure,
came "the" letter to me—"it is unwritten"—and in the
next mail one for Mother; this time, after 2 weeks, a letter
to Mutti saying nothing and for me not a sign of life,
nothing, not even a postcard, a greeting.

But why, why? Why is happiness so short? I surely
haven't become another person in 2 months, and if he
thought me worth loving then, why today no more?

All the remnants of my pride rear up against the way he

has treated me. Am I a plaything that he uses now and then leaves carelessly aside?

Does he feel so superior to everything, so grand, so aware of his invincible power, that he thinks he need not say a word to me when he appears as a stranger? And that last kiss of his was certainly more pity than emotion, it was so frosty too.

No, no I must not yield to any deception, though it be ever so sweet. He no longer understands how he could have loved me.

It was so beautiful, how happy I was with that over-flowing joy in my heart.

And now how colorless life is.
But I wouldn't have missed it. And so I should
surely not complain.
A child that has got chocolate and, instead of
    saying thank you,
cries because it has got so little.
Does this resignation come from my heart?
I think not, no, I know it is not
my real feeling.
I thirst for life, I thirst for love.
"At the banquet of life, barely begun,
for an instant only my lips have pressed
the still full cup in my hands.
I am only at springtime, I want to see the harvest;
and like the sun from season to season
I would achieve my year."*

One joy there is, only one: dancing. And I danced yester-day, and forgot everything. But then it comes again, the grey ghost, that crushes the nerves of my life with its bony hand.

---

* The last six lines are in French. [Ed.]

and the finest in springtime and love
is that sweet, that foolish word:
oh, would it but stay so forever.

27 March 1904

One step further.
My pride has conquered love.
If at least he hadn't led me about in the evening
with an arm around me.
Doesn't he know how offensive and coarse
that is if no feeling inspires it.
He treated me like a strumpet
and I, I let myself be treated thus.
For I, I did love him, but he?
Where is our pride, when we are in love?
And yet I would rather have bitten off my tongue
than say to him: "I'm so fond of you,
what have I done that you act so distantly
toward me? Do you not love me
any more?"
O you, how well I can hate.
Watch out!
Love—hate, *one* emotion really.
Indifferent toward you I cannot be.
My pride now forbids me to love you, and so do you.
What remains for me but hate?
There is probably no soul behind those youthful,
beautiful eyes of yours?
And Karen would only have fallen in love
with your pretty face.
O you, you, you, I will not think of you
any more, you mean, mean man.

Herod and Mariamne

I wept with ecstasy, wily old theater-goer that I am, as I left the theater floating in the highest spheres. Frau Doree, it is true, would probably make every play appear as something significant, she, the only great artist. And beside her Frau Elmenreich! A sight for the gods, these great actresses, to see them competing with each other for the prize of victory. You should stand there, like Goethe and Schiller, handing the wreath to each other.

And the play was in the highest measure worthy of this performance.

29 March 1904

Today again the great longing for him, for his love. I believe I will hardly be able ever again to love someone as I love him, with such boundless devotion.

> "Our love is dead, our love died
>   I don't know how—
> and my heart is heavy—
>   I loved you dearly
> as the strength of your longing courted me."
> But I have grown calmer, calmer and older.
> So wise and so gentle, so understanding of others'
>   troubles, in short, so old.
> But acquit you I cannot, Schorschi.
> Yes, if you had only been flirting with me and
>   philandering,
> but it was more than that, it was a melting of two souls
> into each other, it was love.
> And you owed it to this love—but why go on and on
> brooding over it.

I know I shall get no further that way, and yet I must
ponder over it, ponder, always ponder.

One thought keeps recurring with insistence, but I try
with all my strength to push it back, because it would rob
me of the "belief in the nobility of a soul": he is superficial, and in addition, he is a man. If I accept this, his behavior is very clear to me. If I were beautiful I would say
he was enraptured by his senses and that confused him.
But I am not even pretty; so it must have been something
purely intellectual.

Or another thing—not less painful than this first: he
came to us still almost a boy. I was perhaps the first girl
he got to know, and so he fell in love. During this winter
he may have come to know other girls, perhaps the sort that
would have taught him to despise women. But now enough
of this tormenting. Soon I will probably not think about
him any more, and I will be able to smile at all this heart-
breaking sorrow, and reread on occasion a page or two
of his letters as "fond remembrances," perhaps even the
first one. The wound is still open now, it still hurts when
I touch on it ever so lightly. Then it will be scarred over.

Reinbeck, 14 April 1904

The calm I had been imagining has now really descended
upon me with its black wings full of compassion, so that
glaring rays of sunlight do not dazzle me. But it is far too
kind to me, for not even a stirring of blessed life penetrates
the stillness.

Yet I am too young, too vigorous, for this first blow to
break me. My blood did indeed flow sluggishly after the
great loss, but it is already beginning to pulse more
rapidly.

But often I have such a cramp about my heart that I would like to cry aloud, imagining that I cannot endure it any longer.

And yet it had to happen this way. I am no longer wracking my brains. *Je comprends; et tout comprendre, c'est tout pardonner.* ["I understand; and to understand all is to pardon all."] He is one of those rare people who does everything instinctively, everything, and loving too. He doesn't reflect about himself, nor about his actions, still less about the effect his actions may work on others. A big child?

There is something healthy in him, adorably healthy, unspoiled by modern self-examination *à la* Maupassant, but also something cruel. But then children are cruel too.

Now the ardent longing for love is in me again:

Pray with fervor on your knees:
give us love, Aphrodite.

But it has become more intense because I have once tasted of its sweetness. I often tell myself: this power and strength of love, that is in me, must not be allowed

[Here a page has been torn out.]

Reinbeck, 26 April 1904

I am gay, animated, find good entertainment in discussing the theater or any other amusing subject, I laugh at a stupid joke, make some myself—and suddenly, quite suddenly I am as if paralyzed. Your youthfully lovely image has appeared before my eyes. I need support, I feel so weak and close my eyes tight to prevent myself from crying aloud with pain.

It must be like this when someone who was dear to us

dies. At first we go on living with him, we talk with him, think with him—but then so alone, alone, and this not being able to grasp that one has lost him. And yet that must be easier. It is an iron necessity to which one must submit.

Last night I dreamt about you. You sang:

once I was indeed your love,
in May, in May—
but now it's all gone away.

And looked at me with such a cruel smile. Your features were distorted with scorn.

I woke, and I wept bitterly for a long time.

Reinbeck, 29 April 1904

The question of ethics in free love as opposed to marriage is really nonsense.

Real, deep love is always of moral greatness because it elevates us inwardly.

There is no question that a woman who gives herself freely to a man—aware of the step she takes and all its consequences—stands infinitely higher than the thousands of girls who marry the first comer in order to marry.

When will we stop judging people by what they *do*? What they *are* is the only criterion. For not all people are so harmonious that their actions give the clue to their natures.

Altogether too absurd, judging a person's character exclusively from his attitude toward sex. Much more important is, for example, his attitude toward the truth. Nobody will declare that I am immoral—and yet I could drown in the ocean of my lies.

[81]

The first moral law: thou shalt not lie!
And the second: thou shalt free thy self from convention, from everyday morality, and shalt think through the highest commands for thy self and act accordingly.
Too much custom, too little morality!

Reinbeck, 30 April 1904

I have written to him. I don't want to be small-minded. Written just as a friend, of course. Will he answer? If not, he is lower than I, because he does not distinguish between flirtation and friendship. Well, we'll see ———

Reinbeck, 14 May 1904

A card, picture postcard from him. It had already grown so quiet in me. Now all upset again.
    A picture postcard! Oh, I wish I were able to laugh, laugh so that those who heard it would startle with fright.
    And then—I am ashamed of myself—only to look at him once more in his luminous young strength!
    Oh you, you, what have you made of me?

Reinbeck, 16 May 1904

A letter, calm, kind, friendly.

[Here follow many pages with poems by Schönach-Carolath, Rehtz, Grete Masse.]

Reinbeck, 25 July 1904

That the image of a person whom our whole being once hailed with joy can grow so pale in us. As you went away in the train, in March, 4 months ago now, it seemed to me that my whole radiant young joy of life went with you. Then at first the desperate pain, I believe there was not a night that I didn't cry myself to sleep, no hour in which I did not long for you, no object in the house, no path in wood and field that did not remind me of you. And I was always brooding: why? how could it happen? Until I understood. Then I grew calmer. At times I still felt the pain, when a clumsy hand touched the wound, but gradually it grew quieter, always quieter. And now? —Dear remembrances!

> And I have so much to thank you for, Schorschi.
> With your kiss you wakened me to life.
> You gave me a span of happiness, you
> gave me the depths of suffering, you lifted me
> out of my childhood.
> I thank you.
> You opened my eyes to the puzzling
> labyrinth of my own being, you taught me
> to feel my own strength—
> I thank you.
> For many more the sun of happiness
> will laugh out of your eyes. Oh never let your eyes
> lose their sunny sparkle, you creature divinely endowed!

Fourth Diary

1904–1907

18 Years Old

KAREN IN MEDICAL SCHOOL

∿∿∿

IN THE LAST DAYS of August 1904, Sonni, Karen's mother, separated from her husband and moved with Karen and Berndt to Bahrenfeld, a small town at the periphery of Hamburg. No mention is made of these events in the diaries. Sonni took in boarders; one of these was Ernst, who stayed with them only from July 1905 until the middle of August of the same summer. Toward the end of that year, Sonni and her children moved into the city of Hamburg.

Karen graduated in March 1906 from the Gymnasium after having passed its final examination, the Abitur. She left on Easter Sunday to enroll in the medical school of the University of Freiburg, where the semesters ran from Easter to the beginning of August and from mid-October to spring.

On July 14 of this first semester, she met Losch, also a medical student, and the little Hornvieh. Hornvieh was the nickname for Oskar Horney, her future husband. He was not little, but Losch was taller. Immediate friendships developed. At the end of the semester two weeks later, Oskar left to study law in Braunschweig, and a meaningful correspondence with Karen began. The fourth diary and Karen's letters overlap in time. They share the period of July 1906 to June 1907, but they tell of different experiences.

In August 1906, Sonni moved to Freiburg to make a

home for Karen and herself. She took in two boarders, Losch and Idchen. Idchen was a friend of Karen's from Hamburg.

Reinbeck, 11 August 1904

The close of last year gave me the accolade. It was the first time that I experienced the supreme happiness of being in love. It came over me like an elemental force, like a storm. There was no reflection, no hesitation. No reflection upon what I was doing and ought to do, only total giving to an immense emotion.

It came overnight, came creeping like a thief. I remember that on Christmas day I lay in my bed in the evening and asked myself, doubting, whether Schorschi was fond of me too? For I was fond of him, that I knew. But that that was love, the dawning of young first love's happiness, didn't occur to me. I had indeed yearned madly for love, my whole being dissolved in this one great longing, but it had been purely abstract ecstasy, not such that I would have looked at every sympathetic person in the light of whether he would bring me the fulfillment of my deepest, most ardent wishes. And then on the next day, as he covered my tear-stained face with kisses, as I kissed him, it all seemed a matter of course to me, so natural, as if it had always been so. And the next day in Reinbeck was full of dreamlike happiness, I was so blissful, so divinely happy in my half unconscious enjoyment. And he too was happy. He thought of eternal love; I didn't want anything but the moment and didn't think of the future. I saw our happiness with remarkable common sense as the work of a moment, of which the next moment would rob me.

Irony of fate. He, the sunny creature of the moment, only led by his instincts in barbaric health, soon lost sight of

[88]

my image among new impressions and I—I thought only of him the whole long winter, every minute, every hour. The entire winter was just a waiting for his return. I never doubted for a moment that his feelings toward me were unchanged. And then he came.

How I was able to endure this sudden collapse of my heaven of happiness I do not understand.

He came to me cool and friendly.

At first I was perplexed, I didn't understand. Then the despairing pain, my whole being seemed to be upset. Often most passionate outbursts of pain. Never by the flutter of an eyelid did I show him that I suffered. And he in his healthy egoism never thought that he was causing me pain. It is good if we can vent our suffering in passionate outbursts, for we haven't the strength to hold out long. So exhaustion set in for me too, a dull apathy, and my inner despair broke through less and less often, either in frivolous jesting with my most sacred feelings or in sobbing and weeping.

And then love died in me, quite slowly, slowly; at first I tried to kill it, calling on my pride to help; then came the time, the grey, monotonous time. And after four months I had kissed another. That sounds like a harsh dissonance, but during those days a string snapped in me that has not yet been mended. Am I already in love again? Can I still love? Can one give one's whole heart away twice? Is there a difference between loving and "being in love"? Or is there only the one great red flame that burns our souls? I love you like a sister, Rolf, like a friend who only wants the best for you. You say that my love gives you peace. See, I come to lay my hand on your poor tormented heart. I am too young for other feelings not to be mixed in with this pure love. Then a consuming longing for you comes over me, a wild turmoil of my senses.

But that is just like a foreign element that doesn't belong to me, and it soon disappears.

Reinbeck, 12 August 1904

A narrow army cot in a little room. Raw bricks and wooden beams in the ceiling, two dormer windows at floor level—and yet I feel so rich and safe and calm. For I know that my friend is thinking lovingly of me before he goes to sleep, as I am thinking of him.

and my heart has but a single thought,
you and your happiness.

Reinbeck, 27 August 1904

Took up Ellen Key* again. It's like a bath in the sea in autumn, when the cold is cutting and you have to battle with wind and waves, but once out you are refreshed and a new person. "The old is gone, see: everything is new." For very strong, independent natures it may make no difference what they read—for weaker ones, for me, that's not so. Certainly development takes its quiet, steady way, and yet I would like to persuade myself that I can smuggle in some cooperation of my own into this unalterable fate, by undertaking, for example, to read only such elevated books. But this very wish to be ennobled is probably also deeply ingrained in my character.

Should I now, perhaps, solemnly declare as a last consequence: there is no "free will"—long live slogans!—so we can just drift along, and there would be no need to ponder: shall I do this or do that?

---

* Ellen Key, 1849–1926, Swedish author who advocated political and educational equality for women as preparation for motherhood, which she considered their primary role. She was opposed to equality for women in competitive occupations [Ed].

No. Because we simply *cannot* live without reflecting. We are conditioned in our behavior by disposition, by upbringing, milieu, spirit of the time, and a hundred other forces.

But to come back to Ellen Key, she really is a great person. I too am pervaded by the same deep moral earnestness that is hers. I feel uplifted, happy, when I read her. For her high idealism finds an echo deep in my nature.

How is it possible that from time to time the most brutal naturalism also seems intelligible to me. Are there so many wrappings over my heart that I cannot find the core? Can I read so little in my soul? Or has it so many strings that can be sounded? When I awoke and began with childish awkwardness and joy in discovery to rummage about in the secret corners of my heart, I soon thought I knew everything. And I lay down contentedly and went to sleep. A sweet dream enveloped me, bore me into a white temple with high columns, and sat me down at the feet of a young spring god, and I listened to the gentle motion of the shining sea, a laughing sky above, so blue—so blue. And then Spring laid his hand on my heart, which beat toward him—and it stood still, quite still and it hurt so that I had to cry out.

At that I woke. My blood was chasing feverishly through my veins, my heart hurt so, and then I cried, cried a lot, and when at last I opened my eyes again, the inner spaces seemed so strange that I couldn't feel at home there. Then I began again to search and to investigate—and that's what I'm still doing today.

But my heart doesn't want to move in the old rhythm again. *Na, ça ira.*

Maria by Peter Nansen

Peter Nansen calls his work "a book of love." A phrase of Nietzsche's seemed to me to shimmer all through it: "*Der Frauen Ehre ist Liebe*" ["The honor of women is love"]. The more completely, unrestrainedly a woman gives herself to the man she loves, the higher she stands. The author particularly attacks the notion of preciousness which is taught to a girl (but surely the originators of this market-place morality are men). Thus he once says: "If a girl told me she loved me and pouted at my amorous desire for her, I would leave her as someone unworthy." Thus he has only one point of view from which he looks down on all things: brutal, masculine egoism. Consequently the book is one-sided.

But many pretty pictures, always long drawn out, without any apparent connection with the narrative.

Many fine remarks about women. Beautiful expression of sensual pleasures. Bold disregard of all limits of morals and morality without, however, showing moral seriousness. This "book of love," freed of any brakes of reality, is like an idyl from another world.

Ellen Key
On Love and Marriage

If sometime in later years I ask myself who in these years lit the sacred flame of enthusiasm for me, who was the lustrous star toward which my soul directed its way, one name above all shines before me: Ellen Key.

All I have been thinking about "love and marriage" in recent years, all I have won for myself in ardent battles, all this she sets before the world in radiant letters. What I saw and understood in mute forebodings, I see in her in bright daylight.

Ellen Key is a "believer in life."

She once expresses her ideal:

"If every life is looked upon as its own end-in-itself, from the point of view that it can never be lived again and hence must be lived as fully and as greatly as possible, if every personality is weighed as a value in life that has never yet been and will never be again ———" etc. Her views on morality are determined on the one hand by the individual's demands for happiness, on the other by concern for the species.

Baruch Spinoza, 1632–1677
Ethics

The central point of ethical living is self-preservation. Only through itself, because it owes it to its own persistence, does the mind arrive at happiness; only what its own strength wins for it should it recognize and strive for as the highest good. The mind's only possession is thinking, is reason. Its goal is the truth. Hence happiness is the same as striving after the truth. For the truth is eternal, and the greater our striving, the greater our happiness. This is easy to understand, for happiness is absence of all influences from outside that threaten self-preservation.

An existence is defective, on the other hand, where outside influences predominate. Where intellect is hampered by passion, suffering remains. Thus the desire to please, voluptuousness, intemperance, greed, sensuality express surrender to the force of external things. There is suffering too if the mind strives for something transient, changeable, or when its noble striving attaches to perishable things.

Only one who lacks true insight can suffer in this way. For true understanding brings about moral behavior. This moral behavior must not be the result of fear and hope, for then the mind is in bondage. Hence for Spinoza: understanding is the same as will.

Most people stand under the command of their desires. There exists a common life based on reason (striving for self-preservation) in mutual peace and security—the state.

The church is only for the guidance of souls not yet of age, but the morality at which it aims is of great ethical value, because passion is its driving power.

Every honest action toward which the state works is automatically present in those who live according to reason. And indeed: the more a person strives to maintain himself, the more virtue does he possess. Such a person possesses moderation in place of self-indulgence, reflection, thoughtfulness, or consideration in place of anger. And yet he feels freer through the state which protects him in his external self-preservation.

Knowledge based on the senses alone is insufficient. To let oneself be influenced by imagination alone is also insufficient, because then one's own comfort becomes the yardstick of things. Superstition comes up. It reaches its peak in the idea that the world was made for man's sake, that all things in Nature are just means for man; the world was made by supernatural beings, and that everything dreadful is a means of punishment by those beings, is decided upon by those powers, and therefore is beyond man's conceptive power.

The significance of things must be considered independently of human preference and pleasure, of coincidence and sensual perception, as it is done in mathematics. Reason seeks what is common to all things, the permanent. Its subject is Nature, and in Nature are necessity and lawfulness. From a given cause comes a given effect. All knowledge demands that the causes be sought for. One must first assume a cause; it is the common element in all things, God. God is simply eternal existence, his essence is necessity and eternity. His power consists not in his ability to act now in this way, now in that. He always has will and understanding. Our understanding strives for insights, our will decides. But for God there is no deciding.

The totality of things that offer themselves to our understanding, things in their being and essence brought about by God, is called Nature. Hence God in his unity is Nature.

Divinity as such is hard to grasp, but is to be recognized by its characteristics: the one intellectual, thought; the other physical, extension.

Bahrenfeld, 18 September 1904

I have reached the impressive age of 19. With assurance, I can state that I am completely satisfied with this past year.

I have lived and loved.

Have loved? The tense might not be quite right. For my heart is so heavy today, and only something that is full can be heavy, *ergo*—it was sympathy that first compelled me to be fond of Rolf, then came weeks in which I dissected my feelings for him most scrupulously and in which I wavered between indifference, friendship, and love. Now I have arrived in calmer waters, I know and feel: I love him. —Nothing more. A feeling of deepest security, of rest.

I have infinite confidence in him. He is true through and through, and I must be true toward him too. I can give myself to him quite openly, just as I am. He is my friend. He confides his cares and plans to me and I my worries to him.

And why is my heart so heavy? In three weeks I will shake his hands for the last time, for he is going far, far away to the south. His muse, music, is drawing him away, i.e., in plain German, he is following his singing teacher to Graz. A piece of my most fundamental self will go with him. The thought that he will love other girls does not upset me, only that I shall miss him. It will seem to me that I have become homeless. Other girls—if only they are really good to you, Rolf, and do not drag you down. But that is probably difficult in his case. He is too pure from the ground up, too much the enthusiast and idealist. And if someday he is a great singer and I am a doctor or whatever Nature has in mind for me, then—perhaps—one day we will stop in the street, a familiar face, who?, and suddenly joy lights up our features and we shake hands————.

Bahrenfeld, 15 October 1904

I keep thinking and thinking how to help.

To go away with him for a year among simple seamen, farmers, and work there in fresh air among plain healthy people, as a cowboy if need be, perhaps. But he won't have the necessary strength for such a decision. And with his melancholic way he won't be able to dismiss things from his mind.

That is just the worm that is always gnawing and boring.

Not *what* he reproaches himself for, that he is inept and depraved by inheritance and upbringing, but *that* and *how* he reproaches himself for it, is the critical question.

Berndt says the most consistent thing he could do would be to put a bullet through his head, and in Rolf's place he would not wait much longer, for the waiting only costs money. But that is so desperate, so horrible—and why all this after all? Is he mentally deranged? No. Has he fallen victim to any tormenting fatal disease? No. No, no, it is only that unhappy temperament that is tearing him to pieces. A little bit of lightheartedness, rough vitality, and Rolf could lead a happy life and make others happy. A phrase of Thomas Mann's comes to mind: "There are people who of necessity go astray because for them there is no right way."

Bahrenfeld, 8 October 1904

Three days and he will be gone—forever—my head is in a whirl, I cannot grasp it. And yet of course, I have known all along that we would have to part this month, but now so suddenly—I can't think—how desolate and purposeless everything will be when he is gone.

Cry, sob—I can't; I just stare before me as though to recognize the black ghost of parting, to press it to me—oh, how cold!

I'm so alone; why can't I be with you, Rolf, these last hours?

You, you.

That one wearies with suffering—I understand that now.

And then comes something else again, something new, joy, exuberance, pain, all tearing past us in a tangle, pell-mell, roaring and whistling and howling like a whirlwind, faster and faster, till our sight is dizzied. Oh, you thorny crown of suffering, I press you on my brow and hardly feel that you prick my skin until it bleeds.

Bahrenfeld, 11 October 1904

at 19

Rolf is gone. I stare at this simple sentence and cannot grasp its meaning. I did not weep, I was not desperate, but I felt so stupefied. I see everything as in a dream and cannot understand it. A shudder of a presentiment of death breathed on me. Here we both are and have loved each other, and now suddenly for the last time—will we ever see each other again?—we shake hands. And he, who is now a part of my self, vanishes completely out of my range of vision, and perhaps I shall never, never see him again; all that is as unreal and as inexplicable as death.

Bahrenfeld, 21 October 1904

In these last days it has finally dawned on me what it means to say goodbye. In the first days after he left I experienced only a dull feeling of lacking something; not till a week later did the full realization of the dreadful "Never, never again" come with full force, and with it the longing, the impatient, desperate longing. I flung my arms around the wooden beam in my attic room and sobbed, I lay before my bed and buried my head in the down comforter to choke my sobs. Paralyzing fatigue and apathy.

Then today we had some good news, a prospect of permanent boarders, and my vital spirits rose again energetically. I think this: when one is happy and in good spirits, one can be alone, or in the company of other talking creatures; but the black hours can be brightened by the glances of a friend. And more than that. I am grateful to Rolf for so much. He was my better self. With his idealism, his touchingly impractical sincerity in his dealings, even where it cost him some sacrifice, with his pride, he awakened everything that is good in me. He provided an effective counterbalance to Berndt's utilitarian morality, which was gradually beginning to infect me. He let me take a deep look into his young soul, and through him and his circle of friends he gave me tremendous intellectual stimulation. Even a little bit of an understanding of music!! So I became more mature; also through the fact that I was often worried about him and above all because he aroused my senses. And all the many happy, more than happy hours, the infinite happiness of loving and being loved. Yes, and there is another thing I've learned: to telephone, ha, ha!! Yes Rolf, I owe you many thanks, and for one more thing from which you abstained. For you knew full well that I was yours if you had wanted it.

Bahrenfeld, 5 November 1904

Today I read that first letter of Schorschi's again; I had not dared to touch it because I feared inner revolutions. Yet a curious feeling rose in me today, a flutter of happiness at first, because he had loved me so much, and then suddenly a feeling of the deepest bitterness, as a picture rose before me:

Landscape in March, little villas and to one side a brown heather-covered hillock; we two at a railway crossing. And he remarked so casually: "That first letter was never written." And I nodded smiling, as though that went without saying, but inside me something tore in two. —Now Christmas is coming again soon and by the Christmas tree lights the old pictures will rise before me again.

I believe that the feeling that binds me to Rolf is much deeper, more valuable—but it is not that elemental passion, or only rarely so. Rolf is my friend, my only, my best one—that says everything.

Toward Schorschi I feel as woman only, toward Rolf as human being—if indeed this division is possible for me, which I am inclined to doubt. I think about Rolf all the time, whatever I am doing, and thus I never feel alone. Often, quite suddenly, I see him vividly standing before me —but only for an instant—then the vision is gone again. Now I can well understand how the Ancients beheld their apparitions. —I'm always terribly glad to get his letters, and if the mail doesn't bring the expected letter, I feel suddenly quite weak and miserable.

Ha res est ["Thus matters stand"]

Karen

[A letter to Tuti, on a loose sheet lying in the Diary, had obviously never been sent.]

31 December, 1904

My dear Tuti,

So now I'll begin again.

Today is New Year's Eve. This last year was very important for me. And its final close brought me a gift from heaven, a friend. May I tell you a little about her?

Rolf and I often went to lectures, on club excursions, etc., and almost always his friend Walter Singer (brother of Berndt's friend Paul Singer) was there too with his friend Martha D. —Although the 4 of us met socially occasionally, we did not become very close, as you can imagine. I'm not supposed to go to her house. I could not convince Mother of the silliness of her prejudices. Martha comes from quite simple circumstances, her father is a warehouseman and, it seems to me, the philosopher among the workmen. Martha was at first a housemaid at the Singers, where Walter noticed her because of her extensive knowledge and her thirst for learning. Then she was a salesgirl for a while, and now she is at Grone to be trained as a clerk. She is a fine person, has enormous energy and self-confidence, is clever, has temperament and is kind, very kind. As we were sitting there in her little room and she told me about her rich life—it was already 11 o'clock, we hardly noticed it— I couldn't help giving her a kiss, and now we say "Du" to each other and are friends. Naturally, I feel that there is still much that separates us because of the fundamental difference in our courses of development and our milieus on the one hand, and the difference in our characters on the other.

She writes too—inevitably—psychological sketches. Now you will probably say that I too am always doing something different from other sensible people. Real class differences do not lie in money but in the development of a cultured, educated mind, and in this regard Martha is far superior to most girls of her class.

It is a frightful shame that she cannot come to our house, and Mother can take no part in this new happiness, but trying to convince Mother of the senselessness of her prejudices was fruitless. But this is probably a natural course of events. It is not only the right but the duty of the child to seek new, better ways than its parents could, says Ellen Key.

Through this eternal series of conflicts, development goes on.

I really must stop now; I think I have told you a lot of what is important in my inner life right now; go and do likewise. And go on loving me in the New Year, do you hear? A warm ray from one heart to the other is after all the only thing, the best we have.

Winnetou.*

New Year's Eve 1904–1905

In all the bliss of the first drunken ecstasy of love last New Year's Eve, I toasted the new year and proposed good friendship. What did I expect? To be able to go on dreaming that dream of young love? No, it turned out otherwise, had to turn out otherwise. This last year was a good, tough friend to me. It let the budding flowers its sister had handed me wither, and gave me other flowers, not so fragrant, not so touchingly sweet and delicate, no, they were spicier and stronger.

It gave me a friend, and at the end it still laid the hand of a girl-friend in mine.

It gave me the key to understanding the greatness of some of our greatest men: Goethe, Hebbel.

It lit the flame of my enthusiasm: Ellen Key.

And yet: lesser experiences easily disappear when look-

---

* Winnetou, Karen's adopted nickname, is the name of an American Indian character in the fiction of Karl May. [Ed.]

ing ahead and seeing how much there is to know. I will
look and go in 2 directions:

Strength of Will, Self-Discipline

and

deep absorption in the natural sciences and philosophy,
penetrating into the greatest poets and thinkers

—above all, therefore, hard *work*.

Yes, and I long for one thing more: to learn how to
listen to the delicate vibrations of my soul, to be incor-
ruptibly *true to myself* and fair to others, to find in this
way the right measure of my own worth.

Bahrenfeld, 4 January 1905

For the fourth time I have laid down the first volume of
Memoirs of an Idealist with deepest inward satisfaction. I
believe that around 1848 people in general had more
courage in fighting for their convictions. How far we have
retrogressed since those days! In many things we have
progressed, it is true that a woman can at least have her
own convictions in her heart now, and follow them too.
New battles call for our exertions now. Individual freedom
of mind is achieved; we want this freedom for our emotional life and for its expression, freedom not license, for
we feel bound to the demands of Nature. We want to
achieve a new morality.

What she says about love and friendship moved me more
than ever this time. After the holiest love Theodor returns
to her as a stranger—without a word of explanation. Oh,
how I can understand her torments! How uncommonly
unified and purposeful her character is. She does not seem

to know any sensual excitement, any sensual longing of which she would be intellectually ashamed in other hours.

I am glad that we have gone beyond this high degree of consideration for the family. I admire in her too that unity of feeling; probably because her senses do not inflate her imagination—as mine do so often.

I admire her high courage in matters of conviction, for which she shied away from no material sacrifice.

Yes, there is much left for us to struggle for, and *our* champion is: "Ellen Key."

Bahrenfeld, 31 January 1905

Friday: dressed Martha for the ball and admired her properly. Pretty, but an ordinary hairdo. Drove along with her in the carriage. Friday evening very *"downspirited"* [in English]—thought a lot about how Martha would now be celebrated and how she danced—and I, if I were there too?—I am not beautiful and I dance badly.

Saturday: in chemistry class a talk with A. Loewenthal; she has something dazzling about her, yet unsympathetic. I believe she is not true to herself, and it is difficult to get along with people like that.

Sunday: Museum, pictures by Valentin Rutts. He paints everything separately, not like Klinger with his ingenious daubing. Greatly enjoyed it. Admired again the Feuerbach picture—a woman playing the lute—with beautiful fingers and classically peaceful profile.

Then to *Don Carlos, oh dear* [in English]. I had honestly been looking forward to it. But first the acting of Marquis Posa, a well-nourished, well-meaning face, fat and shiny, with rolling eyes, declaiming like a "schoolboy," then the "divine Ewald" left one cold because he *played* rather than was. Only Paul Wegner as Philipp was good. But all this hollow pathos of Schiller sickened me. What are these puppets doing on the stage? Basic mistake of *Don Carlos*: action becomes so complicated in the later acts, that one can hardly disentangle it. I was dead tired afterwards.

A picture arose before me, also from a Sunday afternoon. Fresh snow had just fallen. I come out of *Wallensteins Tod*. Eyes shining. Divine forgetfulness of the earth. I fall 3 times in the snow. Afterward at home sobbed with ecstasy.

Beautiful time, how long since all that has gone downstream. *Monday* I went out with Idchen. She is like a knick-knack figure in the attic, work-shy, frivolous, graceful, coquettish, a strong sense of irony, clairvoyant concerning her own and other's weaknesses.

29 March 1905

To be free of sensuality means great power in a woman. Only in this way will she be independent of a man. Otherwise she will always long for him and in the exaggerated yearning of her senses she will be able to drown out all feeling of her own value. She becomes the bitch, who begs even if she is beaten—a strumpet. It is a different thing if through the muting of all other instincts, the one instinct has become a power in her, i.e., when she is only "female."

Otherwise eternal battling. And every victory of the senses a Pyrrhic victory, bought with loathing, ever deadly loathing afterwards.

And a man wants a woman calm and superior to these low instincts, of whose power he is only too well aware in himself. Everyone loves that which is higher. Whence the old song about the vanity of man, who wants to conquer, always to conquer, who will accept nothing that is given to him.

Deep in my soul arises an alluring vision. Strong men—
in their arms women whose glance and voice make known
an imperturbable inward harmony, who know nothing of
that war to the death in us between fiery giants and icy
queens, between sensuality and intellect.

Amen

Bahrenfeld, 18 June 1905

at 19

A hard battle between reason and senses.

Reason has triumphed.

If reason has recognized something as necessary, then
the will is identical with reason.

"And I am so quiet after the wild play."

27 June 1905

A profound friendship between man and woman, an understanding of their souls, a sense of being at home each
in the other's heart.

Then love emerges. Ardent in its first desire, and yet
beautiful, tender. Only when there is no underlying friendship, when it is only sensual pleasure that drives one toward the other, can love become shameless; then it does
not matter if it hurts the other person, then each will be
contemptuous of the other.

When the first passion has subsided, friendship emerges
doubly beautiful out of the fiery bath. That is the highest,

most enduring happiness that we can experience through another person.

Yet such an ideal friendship does not exclude one or the other "falling in love" with a third person. For the senses and all the lower instincts too want their full right. And perhaps it is better if these demands are satisfied elsewhere, so that the one relationship is kept more immaculate.

29 June 1905

Kisses and caressings without love, inspired only by animal sensuality, are like champagne out of a golden crystal glass in the blazing light of a festive hall, beautiful women with swishing trains and roses in their hair, subdued laughter and chitchat and above it all the undulating of a light, melancholy, dallying music—it is a dance in a white dress on a smooth floor, heavy red drapes and crepe-veiled lights, your feet skim over the floor and every fiber in your body feels them, feels this intoxicating rhythm. A blissful forgetting of yourself and of the world. Body and soul are melted into one.

You are happy in the moment of your enjoyment.

It excites you and makes your eyes flash in greater joy of life and self-awareness.

And then it passes without leaving a trace.

It blossoms like a flower in the
field. If the wind blows over it,
it is no longer there, and you
no longer know its place.

1904–1907

27 November 1905
20 years old

Many months have passed. And full ones too.

From April till August I had my fling. All calmed down. Perhaps is was good that everything wild in me found an outlet. Perhaps I'm a fatalist, or at least in this case. Believe in causality, in guilt. My bumming around cast shadows—days with Rolf in Berlin, a trip to the Heath.

Rolf, yes, conflict between friendship and love.

But I will briefly put down facts:

12th July with Selma G. to Basel. In Giessen, Schorschi met me at the station. I made an impression on him. He was so embarrassed at first, I think he called me "Sie." I behaved naturally with him, like a comrade. Of course, the obligatory bouquet. Still a delight to see him. The old feeling completely extinguished, forgotten. Saw a lot in Switzerland. But too hurried. In Chamonix a sense of the most boundless loneliness. Hence longing for the only person close to me in those days, Rolf. Wrote him this. One day in Giessen on the way back. That *good* Schorschi; a lovely, reconciling, wishless day. Home Thursday. A new boarder (at the house): Ernst R. From the first instant we felt isolated from "the others." He is clever. An intellectual, always heavy, sensible, conscientious, tends to be serious, appreciates poetry. Nothing attractive about his looks, and yet he charms me enormously. Senses ran ahead of love. On the third day we kissed. He kisses well; asked me where I had learned it. At first elemental passion, so much so that I had not become aware of it at all. In this condition the next Wednesday to Berlin. Two days with Rolf. He felt at once my attitude toward him was different. I told him I had fallen in love. He declared that he loved me— necessity of parting. At the word "parting" I was at first terribly upset and sobbed and begged him to remain my friend. He was disconcerted, but remained firm. At his

[107]

place and in the Grunewald painful discussions. I *did* love
him very much but he demanded my full, undivided *love*,
and that I couldn't give him. In the end champagne—daze.

The following Saturday will stay in my memory above
all. We had dressed up, I in a Norwegian costume with my
hair down. We danced and made a great row. Then I was
in Ernst's room for a moment. Afterward he called me and
gave me a sheet of paper with two of Dehmel's poems on it.
"You hunger for happiness, Eva." Poems all about impetuous loving. I understood, had to understand from the
whole solemn way in which he gave me the paper. Then
we sat on the veranda and he read me about Fennimore
and her love for Niels Lyhne. Suddenly a letter arrives. Unfamiliar handwriting. From Hamburg. I quickly declare it
is from Martha. Go to my own room—a half-insane letter
from Rolf. He was in Hamburg. Longing for love and
death close to each other. I must have looked terribly upset
when I went back. Ernst went on reading, but broke off
soon and asked what was the matter. I only shook my head.
He saw I was suffering. Then Walter Singer came, stayed
a while and took me along. At the station Rolf. He was
beside himself, sobbing, his whole body trembling, asked
for my love, would have nothing to do with my being
fond of him, wanted to kill both Ernst and himself. It was
just a few minutes. I promised to see him the next morning.

I was desperate, thought I could hardly bear the responsibility, battled with the idea whether I could not and
ought not to pledge him my love. I bathed; as I came up in
my wrapper, Ernst was standing in his door. Suffering in his
eyes. I passed him, serious, then went back to him and
gave him my hand but didn't dare to look at him. For a
moment I wanted to ask his help, but some good instinct
protected me from doing that. The night was frightful.
Next morning with Ernst to town; I couldn't, didn't want
to take the responsibility all alone and told him what had
happened and what was coming now. He was naturally
protecting his own interests and mocked me for my idea

of a sacrifice. Rolf a little calmer. I got him to swear by his love for me not to do anything silly. At first he didn't want to, but then he did swear to it. Finally he kissed me twice with all the force of his passion and his desperation —and then I left. The tears were running down my face. And yet I was inwardly calm. In the afternoon to Reinbeck. I went back with Ernst, laughing and kissing—and not a thought of Rolf. Feelings become shallow? Or deep, very deep love that pushes all, all else aside?

The first half of August was on the one hand a happy time—daily life, the secret understanding, the deep feeling of belonging together—and at the same time tormenting because we were both heavy with unsatisfied longing. Then he went away. And it was as though he had forgotten me. He hardly bothered about me. From day to day I grew more restless, until the restlessness got too much for me. I wrote him that we had better break off completely rather than let this situation go on. He wrote a very, very kind letter. The end.

11 December 1905

I love Ernst madly. Now I know for the first time that love is a power. I think of nothing else but him and always of him. Often my longing is so strong that I think I can hardly breathe any more.

If he is here I'm embarrassed and unnatural and moody. His love seems to me now a happiness almost too big for me to allow myself to wish for it. And yet I am sick with longing.

13 December 1905

Two questions are agitating me all the time. The one is: Graduation? Berlin? Study? And the second is: Ernst??

The second is the more exciting because, as yet, there is no answer but only the uncertain promise of a growing relationship. And then of course, I am first of all a woman.

How will it happen? Will he love me? With all his power and passion, so that his reason would be silent? So that for once he would have only the emotion and not be an intellectual any more? Will there come a moment when he takes me in his arms and says: come, we two, you and I, we just can't do without each other! Does he long for me the way I long for him?

And if some day I were to know that he loves me?

Perhaps that is the great charm, my not yet possessing his love. I chase after it and no longer ask whether the prize is really so desirable.

I have never loved a man as I love him. But he is really the first one worth loving that I have met. I wouldn't like to become his wife, in any case not now. For I have a great fear that there is still a lot in me that is only waiting for the waking call to come forth. That's the only thing I believe: there's something more in me. Often, it is true, when I see how dependent I am in my intellectual and moral life on my physical condition, and how I lose my self-control, I think that this belief, too, amounts to nothing.

Does he think of marrying me? He has certainly considered it, and I often think: yes. We would then be carrying out the "moral demand" perfectly. But stop: the end!

Ah, if he were free and big, and we could be happy, happy! Our love would ennoble us. We would protect it like a treasure from any soiling. You and I, I and you—and far away the world. But he is not the man for that. He sits inside his armor of conventionality and talks of "walls" against which he cannot bang his head. So small! And my love could be so rich, I could give him so much, I could make him—and he me—so blissfully happy.

I believe that is the most worrisome thing about our present relationship, that I cannot see *why* it has to be *so* worrisome. Indeed, when I picture him in all his heavy way of thinking and of feeling, and how he silences every feeling through his intellectually balanced consideration, then—perhaps—I understand. But why does he have to be like that, just like that? I ask myself, full of impatience. Child that I am!

The whole game of hide-and-seek we are playing now makes me unnatural as soon as I am with him. I once told him that I was going through life in dancing slippers while he was slopping through in heavy rubber boots. Next time: that I was sluggish and often pretended to myself for weeks at a time that I was lighthearted. What is the poor boy really to think of me? What indeed does he think of me now? And what do *I* think of myself? I believe there is a mixture in me of optimism and depression. At times the one takes over, at times the other. But for a long time I have let myself be influenced by Berndt and given the machine in me a more fluent motion than it has by nature. Even when I began meditating about moral matters I was struck by the fact that you can look at every issue from 2 sides: one light, humorous, laughing, and one serious, ponderous. Berndt tried to innoculate me with the first and it has taken somewhat. But it is the second way of looking at life that sounds the keynote. These two views often conflict in me. Also with regard to Ernst. There are moments (or shall I say: there were?) in which I look upon Ernst as a charming amusement.

And so I have something to think about, have this exciting stimulus: what now? I very much enjoy the way we "play" with each other, and all other longings I interpret as being a result of the physical attraction he exercises on me.

Deep in my heart I think—I believe—(oh this insecurity of feeling) differently: our love is something great, it is an event that has entered into our lives. I belong to you, you belong to me. You *may* not trifle away our lives and happiness like this. For our love *is* a *vital question* for us.

I believe he thinks this way and for just that reason is anxiously asking himself over and over: does the feeling go so deep? Do I love her? Or am I just in love? And because he takes it so seriously he comes to no conclusion and, with all his abstractions, will let me slip completely away from him in the end. Do many girls try to be so fair to their "beloved?" Wouldn't most of them simply reject it all and turn from him without understanding? It sounds funny to sing hymns like this to myself, but I really do not believe that many girls can think abstractly about themselves this way when personal relationships are concerned.

Can he empathize with my soul like this? No, I don't believe so. He fumbles, but can't find anything firm. Otherwise he wouldn't have hurt me *so*. I probably live more consciously than he does. Perhaps I am—well expressed—the more highly cultured? I never tire of picturing to myself the possibilities of how "it" will turn out.

Either he will bind me to himself through his love before I go away, or when he visits me in Berlin, or at the latest during the holidays. After that I will be lost to him. I often feel: if he doesn't take hold now, before I go, it is all over; I mean, then I will get over him, gradually, out there in the big world. Perhaps too, our "great love" will quietly and modestly peter out. But I don't believe that. I have the feeling we are not yet finished with each other.

Yes, *how will* it *be*?

14 December 1905

Am I just physically tired after the lecture? Or is it disappointment that he wasn't there that makes me suddenly
so apathetic, so dead, so dull to all impressions, only longing. I tell myself a hundred, a thousand times that it makes
no sense. What do you have of him? But all that doesn't
help, it is there and it stays. And *why* wasn't he there this
evening? He could have known, guessed, I would be there.
Does it mean so little to him to see me?

I believe I do not quite understand him after all, for
otherwise I wouldn't rebel against it again and again. The
simple solution is: he doesn't care about me any more. But
that I *cannot* believe. He is otherwise so aware in his feelings, he couldn't vacillate like that. But then, perhaps it is
just cowardice on my part that I don't want to believe it,
because the hope is so beautiful and so comforting.

16 December 1905

My longing is always growing. I often think he must come,
drawn by the strength of my desire. But he doesn't come.
Today it isn't so much the longing for his love as simply
the wish to see him, to hear him. And yet I say to myself
that I am not content when we are together.

It weighs on me like a heavy burden.

I often think it is a good thing that I have the compulsion of my work. Thus there are moments when I do not
think of him.

It is as if a dark star stood above our love, so that it
causes us only pain.

Mustn't that be love, true great love, which like some

miracle smilingly clears away the eternal conflict between body and soul as though it were nothing?

Or just illusion?

I don't believe so; well, the future will show.

The future!! ———?

17 December 1905

A leaden weariness lies upon me—
and no desire to live.
I can't take any more.
I can't even work, and when I do work
it gives me no joy.

27 December 1905

"It's all over," my head preaches incessantly, and I must say I am at my wits' end—I do not understand him.

We haven't seen each other for three weeks. He was to come today—but his friend had telegraphed, he would come for a few days—and so he, Ernst, does not come to me.

There remains one conclusion now: that I am nothing to him any more. I found a poem in *Falke* [a journal] that keeps going round in my head:

If you take your heart in your hands
and give it away: there, take it, without recompense,
someone takes it, says thanks, and suddenly throws it
    back at you:
I don't want it any more—and for you a world dies.

If I could just free my heart from him. Indeed, I was more courageous when I wrote him it should all be over. —And yet it was not over, and I myself asked him: come. And he did come, too. But after the first joy of seeing each other again the old torment began once more, only much more so, more agitating.

I shall not write him again now—yet I know I couldn't endure not seeing him at all, so I still have the hope, the anticipation, even if I know every time: we'll be tormenting each other. We each other? Or only he me? For it is impossible that he suffers from it as much as I do—for it does lie in his hands to sweep all bitterness out of this world.

He is cowardly—I am now obliged to see clearly what I had already felt in Bahrenfeld. He gave me the Dehmel poems—I know he waited for me to come and say: here I am—but he didn't want the direct, inevitable responsibility for it himself.

The poems—well, that was a matter of how I would take them, and if I came of my own accord—and that too was my business and not his. He might then have been able to say: she threw herself away upon me—or something of the sort. I know he considers this action of his or rather his lack of action as heroic, and surely it became difficult for him, but there is also *much* cowardice in it.

He was cowardly afterward too. Of course in Bahrenfeld he could have had everything quite conveniently and safely—but outside the house afterward—perhaps somebody might have seen us—"stone walls." Doesn't love stand higher than convenience?

Not his, in any case.

But he says he didn't want to impose on me, for he didn't know whether he loved me or not. Yes, very honorable. And for that reason he lets me suffer unspeakably from his uncertainty for 2 months and says afterward: "I felt sorry for you." Am I then just a woman to him and not also an understanding friend? But what good is it for me to be always remonstrating: his ponderous way, his egoism in love, his timidity, his respect for propriety—it always comes back and seizes me and consumes me like an interior fire: the desire, *the—desire.*

31 December 1905

I read in a book by Renate Fuchs:

In woman, searching for the one, the only one, to whom she belongs, who determines her happiness.

Unswerving search. The search leads steeply down but the *pure* woman *remains* pure however far she may fall.

Happy the one who is set free.

It has set all the strings in me vibrating. The searching—the erring but still searching—searching ceaselessly.

And now I know too that my way will go on beyond Ernst—or better, pass him by.

He is not the man to whom I belong. I often long for Rolf these days. Yet I know: neither is he the one who must come. So I stand alone at the end of this year, quite alone. Therefore I am free to search.

Hamburg, 8 January 1906

School has begun. For the last time. Desperately dull-witted. And the pressure. That dreadful pressure. If I don't pass the exam ———! Then I'm finished. Then I can't go on living.

Don't want to.

No, I can't think it through. Everything finished at once. Without having lived, finished.

But I shall probably make it, and that other thought is only like a phantom that leers at me from time to time.

And perhaps I'm just playing with it.

I am clever enough to learn a great deal in life, but not to find my way out of the confusion of knowledge. Where is the person who is to lead me? Does no one hear how I cry out for him? How little Ernst understood me. He did not hear the cry, he did not listen to what is going on in me. Rolf understood it. He told me the last time in Berlin: "You need someone to lead you now. Let me be the one!" —But Rolf was not strong enough to hold me. Was he perhaps ———? No, the one who is to come is not Rolf.

When I look around at youth, at the young people I know, a stupefaction comes over me like a burden. They all have that deep dissatisfaction. And the others, who don't have it, are mostly superficial. Thomas Truch and Renate Fuchs, they are the typical figures; in my eyes, their books are most emblematic for us, us young people, we who are searching for ourselves and for salvation.

And the older ones?

1. Category: Ruins
2. Category: Children
3. Category: Hypocrites or Sleepers

Hamburg, 10 January 1906

I am so tired. I often wish everything would stop. My life is so frightfully purposeless and without content. One person! Is that asking so much? Oh God, how shall I go on enduring this emptiness? I test everyone around me more sharply, weighing them more exactly, and they are all so shallow. Rolf, why weren't you at least left to me? Why did I have to throw you away in the blindness of my love! If

only Ernst had never crossed my path! Then I would not
have lost Rolf, at least not him. At times I think I must
first be quite, quite alone, to be prepared for the one. But
will he come, will he come? —I'm getting quite mystical in
my belief, in my longing.

25 January 1906

I am vegetating. Many changes of mood. But the depression
dominates, the exalted moods are vague. I am not clear what
the reason for this depression is. Physical exhaustion? But
I'm not working much! Pressure of exams? Yes, certainly
in part, and with that goes the unsatisfying work on the
exams. And another thing: the being alone, the longing
for a true friend, for love, for *the* man. That stirs dully
inside me and then bursts out violently. At times I'm afraid
that in reality I'm not yet through with Ernst. Perhaps I'm
longing myself sick for him and don't know it. I don't
believe so. But I recently read somewhere that the unconscious in people stands in the same relation to the conscious
as the entire mass of water in a pond to the greenery
swimming on the surface.

Hamburg, 1 February 1906

Is this love, this inner tumult to go on forever? Does he
only need to appear for the calm restored with so much
effort to fall in ruins again? Can this unhappy love not
die, the way everything else dies?

Do I really love him still?

[118]

And why else this feverish interest in him? One other thing is possible: deep in me is a terrible, a disconsolate emptiness. The sight of him recalls the time when I was happy, when I lived. And it was he through whom I lived. So isn't it natural that my longing to be alive is instinctively attached to his personality?

This is what I am eager to know, morbidly eager:

Do I still love him with the one true, inextinguishable great love? Or does he keep me busy because my heart is otherwise so empty?

Could I now love somebody else and in so doing forget him?

5 February 1906

I was standing alone at a little window looking out into the driving snow. Suddenly a joyful feeling shot through me: if he were to come through the hedgerow now and wave to me with a smile that said: now I am happy because I am with you. And again it rose in me, that tormentingly blissful certainty that I belong to him and only with him feel at home and protected.

At the same time that impatient desire came again, the longing one thinks is unbearable. The longing that asks again and again, "Why not today? Why not at this moment?" Yes, Ernst, I love you. I have fought against this love, and several times I thought I had the victory in hand, yet it always, always comes again and again.

I am distraught. I have tried to make it clear: he is like this and like that, he has done this and that to you. And my love, like an unrestrained child who will not listen to reason, stamps its foot and says: but I love him anyway. And then adds as if in apology: I can't help it; I myself am only pressed and shoved and driven, and I cannot get free.

Last night I reflected a great deal about this riddle, love. And I've come to the conclusion: it is nonsense to say that I love him for this or that characteristic. Love is a blind instinct that at first seems senseless. And I have also at last found the long-sought difference: love is instinct, friendship is choice.

Rolf

I was quite happy when I came upon the idea of writing down honestly for once, quite honestly, without mental reservations, how my relations with Rolf now unfold before my eyes. For I saw in it a satisfying piece of work for me that would fill out the yawning emptiness inside, and then Rolf is still the one who has meant the most to me. I couldn't imagine my development without him, and I would like to hold these pictures fast before the colors fade. I will have to write much of which my self-love does not like to be reminded. But I will say to myself that honesty alone can give my confession value.

I remember it as though it were today. It was the first fine Sunday in April 1904, and the others had put on their light spring dresses. But I went in my black blouse and with a doleful face. The doleful face came from after-pains of my first love, and the black blouse from performing in a "Passion" play.

The Singer family was to come. Berndt and I had gone into the middle of the field and had sat down on one of those many little romantic, flowery ledges, watching the waters on the Bille go whirling past us. We saw 3 people coming. We thought they were the Singers and we called and waved. To our annoyance they didn't respond. Nevertheless, we saw them turn in to our place. We dashed back to the house. We found 3 people sitting in the parlor: Herr Rhetz, the "poet," a girl friend of his, and a slim boy—youth—of around 20, with dark brown, curly hair, snow white teeth, and such a pretty face that I was horrified and dismissed him as one of the gay boys who frequent the

"Jungfernstieg." That was Rolf. Afterward he talked in the front hall with Mother about the conditions under which he might live in our house. I sat down for a moment outside in a corner and listened and looked at him. It didn't work out and I was glad of that for I found him unsympathetic. The 3 then soon left.

That was my first meeting with Rolf. How I misunderstood the little fellow at the time! I thought he had had his hair curled—and what further characterization one would draw from this shameless hairdo is easy to imagine.

I didn't think then of how I was later to rumple and mistreat his poor locks.

A little later he did move to Reinbeck, to the Neissers'. I saw him a few times on the train, but he didn't see me, and I, little idiot, thought, piqued, that he wanted to ignore me. Then one morning as I was sauntering back and forth on the good old Reinbeck platform, he came up and greeted me. We got in together and rode together. From Reinbeck to Hamburg is 32 minutes. I mention this here, for 32 minutes aren't much, but when one multiplies them and also adds the waiting time in Reinbeck and the walk through Repsoldstrasse, it amounts to quite an impressive number of full hours. And in those hours our friendship sprouted and ripened slowly, steadily.

It was strange. Usually I am shy and reserved with strangers, but with Rolf I talked right away as though I had known him well for a long time. He told me himself later that he had been surprised at the time that I had spoken at once of so many personal things. From now on we always rode together when we took the same train. Very soon he would be looking for me on the platform. Very soon I knew the days on which we would be going together and looked forward to them.

Then one Sunday afternoon he came to our house. I must still have been a little nervous, for as a protection I invited Clemens, who knew him slightly. *Good* Clemens! She enjoyed the day so. It was a beautiful day too. We all wandered over to Bergedorf to the market, where we had our silhouettes cut, Rolf and I even on one card. In the evening we went with our boat to the Menschenfresser [a nightclub] to dance. Rolf and I danced, the others stayed on land. We then rowed back alone together. He told me about his depressed moods and was glad that I understood him well because I knew the condition myself. He also showed me at that time a letter from his little brother, who wrote quite desperately about the atmosphere in the family, and I tried to comfort him. I had to face a scene at home on account of my being late, but the seed of our friendship was certainly planted at this time. On the following days he did not come to the station. I was worried and wrote him a card. He answered with a letter, the first in the long series. He had influenza, wrote about the impression of our boat trip, on which he again had been consoled to know that there still were "big-thinking people." We got to know each other better and better. What characterizes the whole first period of our association is, I believe, that he knew more than I and I looked up to him. And that is easily explained. Some ideas had indeed already ripened in me that went beyond "family small talk." But these ideas I had kept to myself. In my surroundings, higher things were not placed above practical ones. And now in Rolf I had met a person in whom the practical was subordinated to ideas, a person to whom all conventionality meant nothing, an idealist, in short, but not of the cheap variety who enthuse over a lot of fine slogans and never get beyond that.

Our conversations were not always of a serious character, however. I remember so well our morning walks to Bergedorf. We were often boisterously gay and romped like two young colts and wrestled with each other out of pure joy. But he always bested me and so always got his way.

From week to week I looked forward more to seeing him. I remember that on those days I took care to be dressed as nicely as possible. In the train we were always making plans, we wanted to take off and spend a day in the open. But nothing came of it. He was too conscientious. He often reproached me for playing truant and said it was wrong of me. He had so much influence on me that I did give it up. Ascension Sunday was a gay day. The Singers came and Rolf. He brought me poems of Grete Masse that I became very, very fond of. We were all in an exuberant mood. We had brewed a wine punch and marched, singing and dancing, in goose-step around the lawn, Berndt in the lead with the tureen and we coming along behind with the glasses.

Afterward the 8 of us went through Reinbeck arm-in-arm, dancing in circles around the good old Reinbeck peace oak. We were all divinely gay—only Rolf was serious and uncommunicative. In order to challenge him I attacked him on the little wood path at Sophienbad. He justified himself: he had a right to his moods, and he didn't like to and wouldn't play-act. One should understand him and respect his peculiarities, instead of trying to press him into the stereotyped mold. We then quarreled energetically, but his view did make sense to me.

He had been telling me a lot about the Free Association of Artists—and one evening he took me along. It was a rather insignificant but well-meant lecture. Afterward we also met Walter Singer. And with Walter was a young girl in simple black, to whom I was introduced. Her name was Martha. We decided to go to a café. I found this at the time somewhat improper, but I naturally went along. To me the evening is unforgettable, how I, in mute admiration, went along with the 3 of them and heard them talk about modern literature, reciting [Theodore] Storm, etc.

We sat at the little table by the window upstairs in the Hotel de l'Europe; Walter read aloud from *Zarathustra*, the sound of which was new to me and gave me insight into an unsuspected world of happiness. It was nothing new to them. I still remember that, as we left, they recited:

The mist is rising, leaves are falling,
pour the wine, the gracious wine!

The day is ours, this whole day,
let's gild it, yes, let's gild it!
The blue days are dawning,
and ere they flow away
we would indeed, my brave good friend,
enjoy them, yes enjoy them.

Afterward I walked with Martha. I was very shy, for she told me many things she knew about that I knew nothing of. She even recited the opening words of the little Jacobsen novella *Roses Should Stand Here*. I was almost happy when we said goodbye. I hadn't the faintest idea who Martha was. She was very intimate with both, and in the end she arranged with Rolf: "Next Sunday I'll come to see you in Reinbeck, for Walter will be away then." The way I was then I thought no more about it, but accepted the fact that the 3 of them liked one another. In the train I told Rolf that I liked Martha very much, and because he was very happy at that I got a little jealous. He told me she was a salesgirl and used all her free time to satisfy her drive for knowledge. At home I naturally gave inspired descriptions of Martha.

The following Sunday Martha and Rolf came rowing to us. I was happy, for I liked her perhaps even more than Rolf. The reception on the part of the others was frosty. Martha has nothing fine in her social manners, one recognizes the shopgirl in her. And they didn't like Rolf anyway—anti-Semitism and the rest. —A big scolding afterward: impudence on the fellow's part to come along with his floozy, etc. After this the boy was as good as outlawed by our family. And as I was on his side, this day placed me in sharp opposition to the others, so that I drew closer and closer to Rolf. When he asked, I told him quite openly the next day about the misfortune at home, though I tried to mitigate the offensive part as much as possible because I could well see his vulnerability. For example, even later I never dared to tell him that the fundamental reason for Berndt's antipathy toward him was his repugnance at his Jewishness. I never could or would talk with him anyway about this racial difference. I ask myself now: did this fact perhaps unconsciously erect a partition between us, so that he could never mean so much to me?

But I am anticipating.

Rolf came to see us one more time. For the time being it was the last time, for Berndt and his retinue, Willy and Just, behaved quite "unqualifiably" toward him.

Rolf now told me much about Martha and his whole circle of friends, a lot of respectable people who left conventionality aside and only sought the truth. His stories evoked a powerful echo in me. I told him frankly how much I longed to get out into that purer atmosphere, how narrowly restricted I felt in this good-middle-class family life. What impressed me the most was his rigorous morality. He unconditionally placed what he held to be right above practical utility, whereas Berndt had innoculated me with a utilitarian morality. He also tried to influence me to the good, e.g., he was morally indignant over my playing truant. It actually got to the point where I then, and for a long time afterward, took a dislike to myself. But that didn't prevent us from beginning almost every morning at the Reinbeck station to make plans for how we would spend the day if we got out at Bergedorf again and pursued our freedom. Naturally I was all for it, but in the end he was just too conscientious.

In July he invited me to go along on a tour with the Free Association of Artists. I received permission because I pretended that Alice and Clemens would be there, and so we started off on a Sunday morning in glorious weather. On the trip to Hamburg we were exuberantly gay. We were alone in the compartment and romped around. —I think on that morning I rumpled up his curls for the first time. Then we strolled over to the Lübeck station. On the way he began to flirt with a girl who was looking out of a window on the second floor, and he threw my chocolates up to her. *Oh dear me* [in English], how angry I was. When we got to the station he remarked that the best of the day was over. I didn't understand it then—now I understand. I felt a stranger and uncomfortable among the many strangers. I learned to know and like Grete Masse. Rolf and I ate alone at noon. I still remember that we did silly things like a couple of children, that he fed me when I didn't want to eat any more, that I found the idea terribly amusing and the waiter probably took us for a pair of lovers. Afterward I became suspicious for the first time when Walter on some occasion or other said to us: "Children, why didn't you stay in Reinbeck and go into the woods alone instead?" From this I didn't draw the logical conclusion that Walter thought we were in love; instead I got thoroughly confused and flustered, because I only dimly suspected but didn't understand or didn't want to. Got on very well with Rehtz on the way back. In Altrahlstedt we 3 couples, Walter and Martha, Rolf and I, Rehtz and Grete Masse, went to Detlef von Liliencron's. He was awfully nice and gay. I quite forgot that he had recently celebrated his 60th birthday, he was so youthfully fresh. When we heard the dance music from downstairs he said we should just go ahead and dance, he used to dance whole nights through in earlier days. But we didn't do that; instead we drove home. Rolf and I had quarreled bitterly on the money question. I found it too embarrassing that he should pay for me. When we got to Reinbeck he took my arm and we went linked together in all peace of mind. That seemed perfectly natural to me, i.e., when I thought someone I knew was coming toward us I quickly let go of his arm. And when the danger was over, my arm willingly slipped under his. He brought me like this nearly to the house. But at the time I was so little aware of the fact that he was in love with me that, when he told me he had come to Reinbeck to be alone, I thought he was referring to me and that going about with me was a burden to him.

Freiburg, 22 April 1906

I haven't had the time to write for a long time. The whole turmoil of graduation intervened. Now I am released from all that and left entirely to myself. That probably sounds nice—but I am mortally unhappy to be so totally alone. I will use my time going back into the brighter past. The pictures of that time should dispel my worries.

On the Rahlstedter tour we had our first "serious" quarrel. The money question—so often later on—created difficulties for us. I couldn't stand his paying for me. As he absolutely wouldn't take the money, I wrote to Rehtz in my anger and my naïveté and sent him 4 marks to please give to Rolf, or rather to "Rudolf." Oh, I still have to laugh when I think of how after that the little fellow laughed as he met me at the Reinbeck station, and wouldn't stop laughing, and always began again as soon as he looked at me. Then in the train he spread out before me an enormous form with an account in which he had artfully figured out that *he* still owed *me* something, instead of I him. Well, finally—in Repsoldstrasse—I had to take back 2 marks.

I had often spoken to him about my longing to get out of the atmosphere of our house, and in so doing had probably let the ardent wish I had to get into his circle show through. So one morning he came and asked whether I would go with him to Martha's that evening because the whole group was gathering there to celebrate her departure—she was going to Sylt. At first I hardly dared accept, because I steered clear of telling daring lies at home. But my desire was too great and so I said yes. At home I said with some beating of the heart that Frl. Banning had invited Alice and me, and I would spend the night with Alice. We met and went out to Martha's. It was a gay evening. Paul Singer and Frau O., whom in my innocence I took for a friend of his mother's; Behrendssöhnchen; Rehtz, whom of course I had to ask not to betray me at home; Walter and Martha as hosts; James Bauer, who entertained with humorous things and performed the student scene from *Faust* with Paul; then the blond fellow with a head like Christ—I've forgotten his name—who tried to explain to us that every poet has his own, quite definite rhythm: all new people and new impressions. I was, I believe, shy but I felt extremely at ease there and on leaving shook hands very cordially with most of them. Our leaving, yes, I still recall it. Several people offered to take me to Alice's, when Rolf suddenly said in quite commanding tones: "I'll take you home!" [using the "Du"]. I was quite taken aback, for we did not use the "Du" to each other. From this Behrendssöhnchen concluded, as Rolf later told me, that the two of us were rather intimate. Well, so we two left, and I much preferred to have Rolf go with me. I even did some play-acting in order to be with him longer: we had to run to catch the electric tram, the last one, and I boldly declared I had a pain and couldn't run. The punishment followed on the rebound: the mood of the walk went perfectly flat.

Quite imperceptibly and of its own accord our relationship became more intimate. Once he read me a letter from his small brother who felt as unhappy at home as Rolf had earlier, before he had with his characteristic tenacity insisted on his staying in Reinbeck for the summer. I expressed my sympathy for him, whereupon he said rather abruptly: "Shall we be friends?" I probably said something about our being so already. The bond nevertheless was strengthened by this. He leaned his curly head against me and I stroked his dear brown curls very gently. We now definitely called each other "Karen" and "Rudolf" and

"Sie." In those days he was my teacher. He opened a new and more noble view of the world before my eyes. By word and example he taught me: you must always do what you think is right, disregarding the outward disadvantages. There was for example a small detail that seemed quite odd to me and impressed me: his mother, whose whole nature was offensive to him because of her superficiality and falseness, sent him a lovely basket of food. Rolf said: "One may not accept any present from people one despises!"—and gave the basket to his landlady. In brief, I had a proper respect for him and was shy when it came to the point of expressing my own opinions. He couldn't stand my hat. I really liked it very much but I tore it up bit by bit so that it was unusable. Then I went out with Alice to buy a straw hat of the kind he wore. Quite innocently I told Alice the reason. She hinted more or less slyly that I was in love. However I rejected this implication with indignation. And the indignation was honest, for in love I was not, no.

Now the story is beginning to get difficult because it plays constantly close to that boundary between friendship and love, or shall we say to that "boundary area," for boundary *there is none.* He filled all my thoughts and speculation. The days on which I did not see him seemed empty to me. Naturally I always calculated with the greatest craftiness how I could manage to see him.

I knew for instance that Mondays he didn't go home till around 9 o'clock because he first had a piano lesson. So one Monday evening Karen informed the family that she was in the zoological gardens with Alice—which she was. Then naturally I took the train with Rolf. It was a wonderful evening. Suddenly, before Bergedorf, Rolf suggested: "Let's walk to Reinbeck!" I, of course, agreed with enthusiasm.

So: *allons enfants de la patrie!* —Poor Rolf had to carry his heavy music, at which he was so angry that he once flung it to the ground. It was perfectly dark in the woods. I was scared and pressed close to him. He told me about

Pagliacci. Everything was so scary. Once I stumbled. He said he wished I had fallen down so that he could have helped me. That evening was marvelous. There was something in the air, but everything was still so inexpressible, just instinctively and unconsciously felt. Of course we lost our way too—and all the awesomeness of a night alone in the woods assaulted us and brought us closer together. We stopped to rest on a little wooden bench at the edge of the woods. There he told me "His Fairytale": . . . A man is standing on a lonely island. All around him bare, inhospitable rocks. Wherever his eye turns, the wide, wide sea. But beyond in the distance he sees a beautiful stretch of land. The succulent green woods, towers, proud and self-aware. The solitary man spreads out his arms. A whole world of desire lies before his eyes. But how to get there? No boat! And to reach the land of desire by swimming? Impossible. He could get there only if he were to drink up the whole sea, the wide infinite sea!

I understood him and was silent. Perhaps I also silently pressed his hand—I don't remember. Afterward I took my hat in my hand to fan the lovely mild air about my head. As I walked along, a poem occurred to me, and as though it were the mouth of my soul I recited it:

> She used to be a lively child!
> Now she goes deep in thought,
> carries in hand her summer hat
> and quietly bears the glow of the sun
> and doesn't know what to do.
>
> This is because the nightingale
> was singing all night long,
> and from the sweetness of his song,
> its echo and re-echoing,
> the roses now have sprung.

It was half past 11 or later when at last we parted near our little house. As we said goodbye he held my hand firmly in his and said: "Now you believe you understand me and you are my friend. But in 9 months you will think as badly of me as everybody else." I laughed at him. And indeed he was not right.

Formality gave way more and more. And then came a second remarkable evening. All of us were invited to the Kraft's. I was bored to death. Then I had a bright idea: Rolf is going on the 6:39. . . . For what purpose does one attend Gymnasium (except for the half-year before graduation)? So that one can plead as an excuse the pressure of studies that are not pressing! So, with much sympathy about my having so much work and much approval of my zealous sense of duty, I was excused at 6 o'clock.

Right: Rolf was there. Would I come to his house afterward? He wanted to play me something. Yes, gladly. —I must insert here that I really had no afterthoughts on this visit to him. Convention never counted much with me, and through association with Rolf the last remnants of "the young lady" had disappeared. Furthermore, I was *much* too naïve and inexperienced in those days to impute any sort of deeper meaning to the visit. So I went, armed with a French book. On the way I bought him a pound of strawberries because I had noticed at Martha's that he was fond of them. Rolf was standing at the window and let me in. We sat on his sofa together and looked over his old letters and pictures. Then he played and sang something for me, including the overture to *Tristan*. I lay on the floor and gave myself up completely to enjoying the music. Then he took me by roundabout ways to the station. He didn't want to accept the strawberries. We set them down on some stone along the road. On this road I realized for the first time that he loved me. Once he took both my hands, saying: "I am so cold, give me warmth!" In the way he acted toward me, the way he held me and looked at me, there was a distinct and noticeable difference. I did notice it, and it awakened a twofold emotion in me. "On the one hand— on the other hand," Ernst would say. But at the time I didn't try to see it too clearly, for I wanted instinctively to be blind.

Mother was already at home, and I had to do a certain amount of fibbing. Of course, if I got a "B" in French at the final exams I certainly don't owe it to that evening. But if I had thought nothing and Rolf probably very little about my visit, other people had not—in this case his landlady, Frau Meyer! Rolf wrote me this with his characteristic overtones of depression. I was furious, morally indignant, and I believe I trembled with every limb. I immediately took pencil and paper and climbed up the hill in front of our house and wrote down this state of mind. I also addressed him as "Du" a few times in the letter, it just flowed so naturally from my pen and I was too excited to make a clean copy. Besides which, I quite liked it that way. That this shared experience should simply fling us closer together is only natural.

So it happened, as it was bound to happen. It was a Wednesday, the 13th of July—we had just started our holidays, when an urgent letter from Wendt came in the morning. I was going to be kicked out on account of a row with Bohnert, and Mother should come to see him. Well, I calmed my Sonni (my mother), and I myself went to see Wendt. Wendt was engaged, for another hour. Waiting is not my passion—how to kill the time? —Oh, we'll go to Bohnert first. Bohnert delivered me a very fine lecture. I tried to make clear to him that there was no personal animosity toward him in my action but that the unevenness of my behavior lay in my temperament—I don't believe this Philistine of Philistines understood. In any case, I became very excited in the heat of battle and began to weep. We then parted amicably.

Then to Wendt. I was soon to see that I had spent my time most usefully, for Wendt at once became friendly when he heard the whole story.

Well then, I lamented to Wendt that I myself knew that

I wasn't any good in school now: either/or—the situation at home, Mother, etc., etc. I became terribly excited, I laughed and cried alternately.

Meanwhile of course I had been calculating that, if everything went normally, I could get the 6:39. Therefore, I was glad when Wendt took his leave and I rushed to the train. —There was Rolf! And I still so excited and restless. Appointment for a walk at 8 at the forester's house. He didn't want to call for me because he didn't want to come at all to our house ever again.

I came at the agreed time. Rolf had hidden behind a tree in order to frighten me. We went to the Lovers' Beech. On the way we chattered all sorts of nonsense, e.g., that we each had on new boots, and that they cost us each 14 marks, and he told me that Behrendssöhnchen, who just happened to be in Reinbeck, had guessed at once that Rolf was meeting *me*. Just before the Lovers' Beech a quarrel arose— I think he wanted to take a stick away from me. We struggled with each other, and suddenly I felt his breath close to my face. Half startled and half instinctively, I put both my hands before my face. He let me go. From a boat passing by on the Bille somebody called out "That's youth" or something of the sort, which made me angry. For the rest I wasn't imputing any significance to the little incident. Presently we sat down at the edge of the wood. The meadow there fell steeply down to the Bille. We chatted away. And came to talk about forbidden pleasures and the enjoyment of stolen goods. He suddenly said: "A stolen kiss is also lovely" and kissed me. Quite shy, quite gently, quite uncertainly.

I was disconcerted and sad. I had the feeling that now a shadow had fallen across our delightful relationship as friends, that something had come in to disturb if not destroy it. I attribute a certain significance to this circumstance. I think I can conclude from it that my original feeling for Rolf was really only friendship. Of course, it had something to do with the senses—every contact between man and woman has—but what brought us together was in the first place a *spiritual* relationship.

The differences are, of course, so infinitely fine, one can only speak of a more or less.

With his superfine sensibility Rolf must certainly have noticed the impression the kiss had produced on me and he asked: *"Bist Du bose?"* ["Are you angry?"] The "Du" was perfectly spontaneous. I said no. I couldn't be angry with the dear little fellow anyway. I was only sad. I think he asked me then whether I loved him, and I only said he must know that already.

He became more and more serious and silent. I tried to cheer him up and teased him. He didn't react or did so quite wearily.

Then we went home—through the middle of the wood. He was depressed, and in a sort of gallows humor told me one stupid joke after another. I could hardly bear to listen, I felt so sorry for him. Once I took both his hands. I wanted to kiss him but I couldn't. Then we went on. It got darker. We sat down on an old moss-covered stone in the middle of the wood. Then I took heart and with energetic determination gave him a kiss. I don't know what *he* felt at that. He was very sweet to me but didn't kiss me again. As we went on, arm in arm, he suddenly brought out: "Snake!" As he told me later, he had felt my kiss had only been given out of pity. We quickly went home then, by the upper road between field and wood, which leads past the cemetery. Then together we ran down the wooded hill. Down below he kissed me goodbye. *Auf Wiedersehen* until Sunday morning! I got home red and hot. Feeling a little guilty, anxious that nobody should notice anything. And yet I was happy. I stood before the mirror and looked into my excited face and saw myself as something new, interesting. How it would go on from here, I never thought.

Willy, our boarder, told me next morning that in my sleep I had called out: "No, I don't want to, I don't want to!" Rolf told me later that he had had fearful qualms of conscience that evening and had been reproaching himself.

The following days I did think about him a great deal, but absolutely not as though I were in love. It seemed to me unlikely that we had kissed. I had almost forgotten it when we met again Sunday morning by the churchyard. He had become much more of a stranger to me since that evening, the intimacy had vanished. I called him "Sie" again, it would have been impossible for me to call him "Du." We walked in the Great Common fields and got lost again. Our conversation was impersonal and meaningless. We sat down in the woods. I had the feeling he wanted to kiss me but didn't dare. As we chased around a bit, my hair came undone and he loosened it altogether so that it fell free. We played together. Naturally, great trouble putting it up again afterward. I had also lost my two best hairpins. The way back went better, we walked arm-in-arm and conversed sensibly. He complained to me about suffering from having so little self-confidence. That was indeed the case and made him irritable and sensitive. We then had a discussion about free will, I think, or something of the sort, until we parted. No word about that Wednesday evening. I remember that I was content about it. I thought he would have forgotten it, like me. Whether this satisfaction was real or feigned I can now no longer tell. The same Sunday evening I met him again at the fair, where he was with the Singers, Rehtz, and others. We went on the swings together. There was some estrangement between us. Around 11 the others went away. We and Willy had a little more free time. So Walter, Willy, Rolf, and I went on together to Reuch's but didn't dance much. Rolf dances horribly. Later the others went on to the Harmonie, but Rolf and I had no desire to do that because it was crowded. We said we would rather go back to Reuch's or take a walk. We did the latter and climbed up the hill. At the top Rolf declared he was tired and we should sit on the bench. That we did. Then he began to kiss me passionately. I remained

perfectly passive. Only when he hurt me did I remonstrate.
I half lay, half sat, and again and again he pressed his
lips to my face and neck. He kissed incessantly, almost as
though he were parched with thirst. And I let him kiss me
—and felt nothing, not the least bit, save for displeasure
at my uncomfortable position and his too vehement passion.
I often shoved him away, said he should stop now, but he
didn't hear me. It was 1 o'clock when we finally got up
and went to fetch the others at the Harmonie. I was self-
possessed enough to tell the two of them what a nice time
we had dancing at Reuch's—Rolf was silent.

Then I went home with Willy. Mother was furious at
our being so late. Next day there were great dramatic
goings-on until Willy had brought his "Sweet Clo"* around
again. Early next morning Walter, who had spent the night
at Rolf's, came to breakfast with me. I took him to the
train, where Rolf was too. Again I felt nothing on seeing
him. But during the day I missed him more and more, so
that in the evening I went to fetch him from the train. This
game went on all through the following period. If I was
with him or had just been with him, I was cool and not
at all in love. Then I tortured myself with doubts and
questions: Do I love him? Do I *not* love him? And usually
came up with a negative result. But then came the "desire"
and away went the questions, vanishing before the one
elemental feeling. But then again I vividly remember our
conversations, when I told him that the plan had succeeded
with Alice's help and we would have all Sunday afternoon
and evening to ourselves. I think he asked what Alice
thought of Bienchen.† I told him that Alice was inclined to
idolize him. At which he said something like: I should be
sure not to do that with him. And the idea seemed to me
perfectly absurd and I laughed at him. Moreover, he came
back to this theme several times and would have been only

---

* A nickname for Karen's mother, Clotilde. [Ed.]
† Nickname of her boy-friend. [Ed.]

too glad to hear from me that he was my "Lord and God," but in those days that was something very far from my thoughts. Well, that Sunday afternoon I really had to be extremely crafty in order to be free. But there still remained that tremulous and provocative feeling of danger. We went into the Saxon wood and lay down among the bilberries, right in the midst of them. So much so that my white sailor blouse was stained absolutely purple. It strikes me that at this time we almost never had any "sensible" conversation. I felt like a stranger to him and shy. It was as though something strange lay between us that had been added by the sensual aspect. We played around there in the bilberries like two happy children. We kissed a lot too. And in all that there was something infinitely chaste and pure. My senses were really hardly awakened—and he is of a nature that is chaste through and through. And we were both still so young, I 18 and he 19. He once asked if he could kiss my breast. Quite astonished and embarrassed, I said no. And he did not press me further. Afterward, as it grew dark, we walked along to the lake by the Aumühle. He was deeply melancholy again and spoke of nobody loving him whereas everybody liked Walter and me. Gone was any being in love—and I was once more the good companion who wanted only to help and to comfort him. *Wanted to*, yes. Oh, so much. But I felt powerless against this deep depression. And that often made me very sad.

I no longer remember exactly how the sequence of our times together ran, from which I conclude that no external, visible development took place in our relationship, only that it very gradually grew deeper. But only *very* gradually. I know I couldn't easily adjust to our altered attitude to each other without having undergone some change on account of it. For although for the most part his kisses left me cold, I did accept them with a sort of passive well-being. And soon I had become so accustomed to them that I couldn't get along without them.

He came to our house again too—persuaded by Walter,

I think—naturally, on an evening when Berndt was not at home. Willy and the others kept to themselves. After supper we two went for a walk on the Great Commons. He sat down on a fallen tree and I sat on his lap. In the bilberry patch I had first called him "Rolf"; now he told me that he loved to hear that name and I should always call him so. He was very gay: at work they had promised him 1,400 marks for next year, and now he had to keep thinking of the 2 things, me and the 1,400 marks. Was I angry that he should think of something else than just me? I answered with a seriously meant laugh. In my thoughtlessness I judged him a little by my own feelings and did not see that the little fellow really loved me deeply and wholly. I probably was too self-involved in those days, with the uncertainty of my own feelings, to be able to bother much about his feelings. And then he did remain the same in his manner toward me. It was already dark when we left. On the way we teased each other and squabbled. He showed an inclination to torment me on that occasion, as he had done before. That evening I think I was very angry about it. We got back to the house with a rather bad conscience. Alice came to stay with us for a week, and—perhaps fired by her glowing sensuality—my feelings for Rolf entered quite a new phase: there was no question of friendship any more, only of passion. By day I was half sick with longing for him. Evenings I often saw him, with Alice's help. Alice warned me to be careful on account of Mother, and for Heaven's sake not to get any further involved with him. I totally rejected the thought of this last danger and was childish enough to deny the possibility outright.

Twice Bienchen came and the four of us went off, officially only three. The first time we went through the Vorwerk wood and the Wohltorfer road. At first we four walked together, Alice and Bienchen arm-in-arm, we two not. Bienchen was terribly funny and we laughed ourselves silly when the two imitated the way a group had sung in Cuxhaven:

Let's be going to the Isle of Love,
It is lovely on the Isle of Love,
All alone on the Isle of Love,
Happy and contented let us be.

Gradually the distances between the two couples grew bigger. But it was indescribably embarrassing to me when Rolf began to get amorous with me, especially so long as the others could see us. But that was not the only reason— he was able on that evening, as otherwise not so often, to inflame my senses. As we came to the Wohltorfer road we wanted to wait for the others and sat down on the roadside. As they came along it suddenly occurred to us that it would be very amusing if they went past without noticing us. So we lay still—and the two really did pass by. So there we were lying alone in the nocturnal darkness of the woods. If I am not mistaken, his amorous attentions were simply repugnant to me, and I let him feel something of the sort. I found that his behavior disturbed the beauty of the evening. It was quite creepy as we at last sought the road back. One couldn't see 3 paces ahead. The evening became still more uncomfortable. At first there was the dilemma again of neither of us knowing what to say to the other. Then he got angry when I began to sing a cheap hit song, and afterward I got angry at him for some reason or other and gave him an honest-to-goodness box on the ear. And then came the worst: Alice and Bienchen had lost their way and were terribly annoyed with us.

Well, we nevertheless went off with the two of them once more, and this time on a Sunday afternoon to Silk. But this time we were so sensible as to separate immediately in the woods. We two strolled around and more than before I had a breathless fear of meeting anyone. I told Rolf, partly of course under pressure of that fear, that we couldn't go on like this very much longer. We had better break with each other. The "young lady" with whom Rolf had so often teased me was expressing herself clearly for the last time. The reaction to the new atmosphere, the fear that Mother *must* sooner or later notice something. And even if this was no definite decision, but rather an "it would be better if," it did bear witness to the fact that I still had a very superficial grasp of my relationship with Rolf. And Rolf quickly talked me out of it. As we began our fighting game again, he once asked: "Are you really not at all afraid of me?" I probably only half understood the meaning of the question. For, even if I *knew* anything about sexual relations in those days, it was just an external knowledge and nothing personal. I replied to his question in the negative, laughing. When we had walked ourselves weary, we went to Silk where we met Alice and Bienchen. Our time together there was thoroughly uncomfortable. Bienchen, probably irritated by the contrast between himself and Rolf, showed the anti-aesthetician in him, the common person. I noticed that Rolf was vexed by it. As soon as we had eaten, we separated again. Rolf and I lay down at the edge of a field against a haystack and dreamily followed the sinking sun.

A serene peace was about us, and within us a deep, wishless, and yet so blissful stillness. For a long time we didn't speak a word. Then Rolf began to tell me the story of Walter's love, "blonde Gretel." And as he told it a great sadness came over me. I thought he too had loved this woman and—perhaps—loved her still. I had the painful feeling a second wife must have when she enters her husband's house and sees herself excluded there from a thousand memories. Again I was shy, strange, and helpless toward him and did not dare lend expression to my own real feeling.

Now that I have again given myself over to the harmonious tones of *Hyperion*, another episode comes to mind which also took place at this time. Behrenssöhnchen was visiting in Reinbeck and often came to see us. One morning Alice and he and I went out. He led us to an idyllic spot, a shady little hollow in the midst of wheat fields, and there we lay, and he read Hölderlin aloud to us. The words went to my heart, or perhaps more than the words, their sound. Women reapers came and bound us with sheaves and recited their little saying. It was a real pastoral play, that morning. Soon after that Rolf took sick, a cold as usual. I was naturally inconsolable at not being able to go to him —he was still living at Frau Meyer's. On Sunday morning I couldn't stand doing nothing. I secretly slipped out to the village gardener and had some red roses cut. Then I went near his house and sent a small boy up to him with the flowers. In the evening he came to us with Walter. With great effort, I captured Beppo to come with us. Walter took command of Beppo-Boy, so Rolf and I could go alone. But I soon regretted it, for his passionate attentions again were repulsive to me. I found it crude of him to kiss me while he had a sore throat—I had been in the mood for a peaceful walk and not for such assaults. But again I was too bashful to tell him so frankly. I simply tried my best to pull away from his grasp. Finally I fled to Walter and Beppo so that he had willy-nilly to leave me alone. Next day I actually had a sore throat too and by evening I was in bed with fever—inwardly cursing the egoism of Rolf who had not thought to protect me. Result: I hardly thought of him during the next few days although I knew he was not yet better, that he had moved, and that I could visit him there. Then, out of the blue one afternoon, an absolutely unbridled longing for him came over me. There was hardly an excuse I could think of for going out, for it was raining in torrents, with the storm howling from every side. I was not fussy. I had to go. I simply declared I had a letter to mail and went at a rapid pace to his place. And there I was, with him, soaked through and through, half happy, half embarrassed, and confused. Rolf was overjoyed at my coming. We sat on the sofa together and chattered and kissed. I had to leave again only too soon. At home I made up a whopper about having had something of a fainting spell on the way back, but I had a rather uneasy feeling in doing it.

I must stress one thing again because it now seems to me rather remarkable. Namely this, that I, who after all was almost 19, went to the person I loved in complete, unsuspecting naïveté. That it never occurred to me to ask: does this visit have a deeper meaning? Can he interpret it differently from the way it is meant? And he did take it the way I gave it. It's possible that he desired me even then, but he left me to my childish innocence, until suddenly— but of that later.

Not very many more details about the Reinbeck period come to mind. Yes, I do remember one Sunday. I had met him at the station around noon and gone with him to Schöningstedt to eat. Afterward I saw him home—then I had to leave. In the afternoon I wanted to go to him again. So I announced that I wanted to take a walk and was "very sad" that nobody at home wanted to go with me. At which my dear Mother said I should ask the village forester to walk with me. To which Karen, as a good young lady replied: "I wouldn't do a thing like that." —And then I went to Rolf. We had not been together long when Walter arrived. He came from our house and said he had thought I would be here. He read aloud from *Zarathustra* about the dance, Rolf played piano. And beyond the window spread the broad fields with Rolf's favorite Böcklin trees and the rim of the woods on the left and the churchyard with the little white chapel.

I left first, Rolf and Walter followed later. One more little detail is in my mind, one that is very characteristic of Rolf. A man passed by with his wife and baby. Mutti jokingly said: "Look there, the picture of your future." To which Walter said with a sigh: "Ah yes, one may run into bad luck." Rolf was simply horrified at this joking remark and told me the next morning that he could hardly believe his ears. One evening Rolf and I were invited to the Singers together. A sort of musical genius, Fischer, was to be there

and play. I was at Käthe's first. She made me a geisha
hairdo which went very well with my flowered geisha
dress. The evening was very enjoyable. Fischer played
Wagner and other things. At 10 o'clock Rolf and I left.
Shrill discord again on the way home. We were probably,
especially he, sensually aroused. There was a young man
in the compartment with us. But Rolf recklessly gave free
rein to his passionate mood and kissed me madly. It really
is strange: as the long series of pictures unrolls before me,
all the hours in which our senses spoke loudest seem to me
somewhat ugly, like a foreign body that had entered in
and did not belong there. And that lies not only in the
matter itself, but I believe that the spiritual part in-
voluntarily appears higher and nobler that the physical.
But when I think back on such moments with the man I
really loved, with Ernst, they often appear to me to have
something beautiful and precious. But it may also be due
to the fact that with him I did not have the finer feeling,
but was blindly craving a sacrifice for my senses. Perhaps another reason lay in Rolf's awkwardness in going
about it: he did not kiss well, he was at bottom such a
chaste nature that he too found himself in strange waters.
And certainly the man must take the sure lead. Only then,
when he is able to, does the woman have full enjoyment.
He must not feel hesitant, he must proceed, calm and sure.
I could add as another reason the fact that I was then more
child than woman—but he could have wakened what was
slumbering in me. I think that something unresolved still
remains in spite of these explanations, and I believe that
it lies in the fact that the *fundamental tone* of our dealings was that of friendship and not love, that it was
spiritual and not sensual. We were naturally often together
but no noticeable development ever took place in our
relationship.

One morning he told me, radiant with joy, that in
autumn he would be going away, to Graz. Everything inside
went into a tight knot but I did not have the courage to

come out with my opinion—and so I only said that I was happy for him, and nothing further. And he didn't seem to be thinking of me in the matter at all. But since an excess of self-assurance was never my weakness, I swallowed that down in silence. It was a very perturbing time for him now because Frau Pennarini was so extremely ill. Once I met him after his music lesson. I had to wait for him, playing with the baby meantime. On the way home he told me beaming that Frau Pennarini had praised his voice enormously and promised to do everything for him.

In the middle of August we moved to Bahrenfeld. Right away on the first Sunday I went out to see him in the afternoon, with a violently beating heart, to be sure, for I might run into my old man.* Rolf met me at the Bergedorf station. In Reinbeck we stole very carefully along the upper edge of the woods to Rolf's room. The woman brought supper in to us. We were standing at the window, looking dreamily out to the little churchyard and at the Böcklin trees that stood out so clearly against the sky. Perhaps in response to the woman's behavior toward me, I said: "I wonder what she thinks of me?" He looked fervently at me and remarked: "And would it be so bad if that were so?" I thought no more about it, for "that" was something unthinkable for me. We ate cosily. Rolf played and sang. We spoke of the beginnings of our relationship, Rolf doubted that I cared anything about him. I reassured him. I wanted to take a train around 9 o'clock. He wouldn't let me leave. When he begged me, I stayed. Then a wild scene unfolded. We must both have been pretty excited. He tried to undo my dress. We fought with each other. He threw me down on his bed. I saw his hotly glowing eyes close to mine. I yelled at him: "Beast!" He stopped. But the game started over again. I can still hear the tone of his voice as he half begged, half commanded: "Karen, Karen, Karen!!" He disgusted me. I did not want to be desired by him. I

---

* Her father was still living in Reinbeck. [Ed.]

had no desire for him. Once in desperation he was insolent: "You'll stay here tonight, won't you?" —I believe I went dark red, anyway I was profoundly ashamed.

Then we went to the train. My hair was roughed up. My dress in disorder. I was so little master of the situation that I was not short and severe with him—perhaps I was still too excited. This was the only time in the Hamburg period that he tried to bind me closer to him.

Another Sunday we went for a walk on the heath. Of course I had had to set up a whole battery of fibs for the purpose. But everything went well. We got into the heather. We soon separated from the swarm of people and lay down in a cosy corner of the woods and kissed and scuffled and romped around like two young dogs. Then on to Wilsede. There, out of consideration for the exchequer, we ordered only sandwiches, and Rolf ordered wine. I still have to laugh when I remember the scenes that followed. He got completely befuddled, right after the first glass. I had to guide him even to preserve a semblance of decorum. I was half angry, half amused, but felt mostly an unpleasant sensation. Luckily he soon sobered up. In Wintermoor another scare. I went into the waiting room with Rolf. Fortunately, we were walking singly, he behind me. There we ran into Rehtz, Hahn, and Clara. I quickly got hold of myself, greeted them beaming with joy and explained that I was looking for my two girl-friends—we had separated because we wanted to try out different paths, etc.—and totally ignored Rolf. Afterward I just managed to get into the train unseen. Meantime we got hungry, of course, and so got out in Hamburg. Rolf was perfectly sober again. I still remember that I was quite excited and longed anxiously for Rolf to kiss me; but, as on other occasions, he did not seem to be so inclined. We then went into a restaurant. We got back home late.

We were not seeing each other so often now. On my birthday he sent me a letter at school. In it he addressed me as "Dearest," told me that the business about Graz was in perfect order and he would leave the middle of October, that he looked back with pleasure on our walk in the heather and had a great longing for me, his "Snake." For the rest, I should appear promptly on Saturday when we were going to *Tristan* together and I shouldn't eat too much birthday cake. That Saturday we sat together listening to *Tristan*. I was deeply moved. My hand sought his, to feel his nearness. Unfortunately, toward the 3rd act I became very tired and was unable to follow the music further.

Hamburg, 18 August 1906

The first semester is over now. Home again. But all this doesn't interest me enough that I would find it worth the trouble of writing it down. Not Freiburg either, in spite of Losch, nor Berlin, in spite of Ernst. I'm only thinking of one evening. Three days ago. Ernst did not come to supper and I was already beginning to dismiss any thought of his coming. I had beautified myself for him—I was feeling bellicose—I wanted to win him in battle. The expectation had made me strangely restless—feverish, combative—and strong. I knew that he meant so infinitely much more to me than the others who have come close to me. He is the only one for whom I can suffer, and that not with any exciting sensation, not suffering for the sensual pleasure of it, but with a suffering that is quite bitter and severe, because I must. By this I recognize how great my love is for him. Well, and then he came. I seized upon him; I went at my goal recklessly. It often seemed to me that under his gaze my words turned into arrows that flew swift and sure. I hinted lightly at our common reminiscences, I took everything more lightly than it was in reality. I treated him like a discarded lover who charms one by loyal regard and remembered sensations. I have never played so daringly. Once he wanted half a lump of sugar in his tea. I took a piece, bit it in two, and put in his cup the half I had had in my mouth. He did not stir the tea but drank it up and ate the sugar by itself. More grace than I had thought him capable of! Perhaps also subconsciously.

At 11 we went to the café. Presently Berndt came, a little high. So the tone changed. Berndt began to flirt a little with Hedi, Ernst with me. Fraternity, spilled beer, jokes. Changed dress, then to Lauer's. Right at the start warning not to make a row. Rhine wine—port wine—champagne—brandy—coffee ———? ———? ———? Then we left. Talked together seriously—that we had remained true to each other, that we loved each other very much. And we kissed. We were very happy, very happy!

Freiburg, 3 January 1907

It isn't really New Year's Eve, but still around the turn of the year I feel driven to a retrospective summary.

This last year—how did it begin? Oh, I know, those were grey weeks—the suffering of my love for Ernst, the pressure of exams. Then the exam itself and the intervening weeks with mostly domestic activity. And then an Easter Sunday—when I went ahead into an unfamiliar life with a thousand anxious expectations.

The first semester—never will I forget those first days here, days full of desperate loneliness, of the disconsolate feeling of being forsaken.

Indeed, not until I made good friends with my little Hans Bender did it get better. And no sooner was it better than I already wanted more, wanted something for heart and senses. So I made a start at it. On July 14th the commemoration of the academic-social society was celebrated at the

Dattler.* There I got acquainted with Losch—and the Hornvieh. We danced a Française together, neither of us knowing it—we threw rose-leaves at each other on the veranda, which was decorated with colored lanterns. There we wrote a jolly postcard to the "Vulture"—we went arm-in-arm down the Schlossberg at three in the morning and out to the suburb of Güntherstal. And suddenly somebody was walking beside us, telling one story after another—it was the little Hornvieh. Somewhat later we sat on Hornvieh's balcony, dangling our legs and laughing at each other, happy and surprised, not understanding our being together there at all. And then it was all the way up the steep road to the Solacker hill in dancing slippers and ball dress. Up there we lay in the sun and gradually our eyes fell gently shut. But we also got more and more hungry, and then it was down again to Güntherstal to eat. Yes, and then I was lying on Hornvieh's sofa and awoke because something was very gently stroking my cheeks—it was the little Hornvieh; but I was annoyed at that, for I was in love with the tall fellow who had fallen asleep among cigarettes and books on the balcony. That evening the two of us sat on the Dattler again. —And he kissed me, and I felt that he was strong and that joy of living and strength burned in his kiss, and I came to love him. The last 2 weeks of the semester we were always together, with the exception of a few nocturnal hours. We drank tea for hours at my place or visited the Hornvieh, or it was an evening of music, or we went walking. All permeated by a serene careless joy of life. The funniest thing was the jealousy of my little ones (Losch and Hornvieh), and how I finally managed to reconcile them by making the tour to the Jägerhäusle. Our being in love, however, developed into a passion whose impact was too strong for us. But then, luckily, the day of my departure had come.

One day in Berlin. Strolling about with Ernst. Wine

---

* A restaurant on one of the mountains overlooking Freiburg. [Ed.]

parlors, the first big binge of my life—taxicab—Christian hostel—and then Hamburg. There my old ardent love for Ernst flamed up again in all its terrible glory. A few hours —no, days—a nameless, blissful, engulfing happiness, then it was all over, and the old suffering demanded its tribute anew. I became so mortally weary then. I just dragged myself along through a paled and empty life. That fellow!

What I suffered because of him. Now at last I am free of him and at rest, for I have seen him too clearly for what he is. Him in his good-citizen's pettiness and cowardice, in his mendacity, in his brutality and his egoism. How could I ever have loved him so deeply, so passionately? Forever an open question. And yet, I know why: he is of the same mixture as I am, the mixture of Rolf and Berndt, only in different proportions.

Then came a few happy days on the heath with Losch. The bond between us became stronger, more intimate—and it became always more so in the weeks of our living together—to the mere *being in love*, friendship was added, *loving*. His strong love for me is something infinitely calming, making for happiness.

But another thread stretches from the 14th of July. Correspondence with the little Hornvieh and the start of a friendship with him. And with that the taking up again of a thread that ran luminously through a year of my life, the friendship with Rolf. What Rolf awakened in me is being brought to life again by Hornvieh. How shall I say it briefly? The reflecting about myself perhaps, about the deeper springs of my ego, the search within.

But, if I were to read this some day in later years, I would get no correct impression of the year 1906 if at least one more point were not mentioned:

I am getting fonder and fonder of my studies and my working power is borne on the wings of joyousness in work.

Freiburg, 7 January 1907

I still want to bring the story with Rolf to an end, though it can only be done in broad outline as I left the letter material necessary for it in Hamburg. It was on an afternoon Rolf and I spent with Walter and Martha that I felt a cooling of our feelings. A disharmony ran—I don't know why—through that day. We did not see each other at all for a few days after that and heard nothing from each other. Until the longing in me grew too strong—so one afternoon I went to town and waited, I think for two hours, in front of his store on the Neuenwall. But he did not come. Yet the next day we met again and soon all those traces of gloom vanished.

On the 1st of September he moved to Hamburg and actually into Walter's future room near the barracks. We had some happy evenings there. I still remember my train arrived at the Dammtor at 7:18 and he was standing downstairs in the hall—I recognized him at once by his brown slouch hat—and then we went to his place. The landlady brought us tea and a rivalry sprang up as to which of us was better at cutting bread. After the cozy meal he played and sang, in those days it was mostly *Tristan*. And then we sat side by side on the lodging's shabby sofa. He often laid his head on my shoulder and lamented about the suffering the encounter with a cold, mendacious world caused him, and about the deep *Weltschmerz* that filled his young soul. And I tried to drive away the black shadows. Often I talked about one thing or another, and often just let him weep in my arms.

Those evenings—when I think back to them a far-from-worldly peace settles over them. There also lay upon them a deep melancholy, for we both knew we would soon have to part—perhaps for ever. Each of us wanted to show the other only tender love. Each would have given his heart's blood without a second thought for the happiness of the other. I once read that to love a person means to wish deeply and ardently for his happiness. If that is love, we fulfilled it perfectly in all its glory.

Those evenings were a refuge for both of us, and occupied our thoughts during the day's monotonous work, among more common people.

On the last evening, before we had to part, he took my hands in his and said: "Do you know, Karen, that you owe me thanks?" Yes, I knew it. I would surely have become his lover if he had so desired. For at that time I could not have refused him anything. On Tuesday, the 12th of October 1904, he was to leave. The Sunday before I was in Lübeck with Berndt at the "Mummy Show." There such a longing seized me for my little friend that upon returning I got out at Sternschanze station on the pretense of going to see Alice, and went to him. He had just left—to mail a letter he had just written to me. He too had been anxious about me. Throughout this letter there runs a moving tone of deep, grateful love for me, grateful because I had safely guided him through the most difficult weeks of his life; one also senses a feeling that my loving him was an undeserved gift for which he could never, never thank me enough. I often had to think of just this letter later on! So he left on Tuesday. I went with him as far as the Klostertor. We said goodbye. I felt as though my heart would break. I had the certain feeling: it will never be like this again, it is over.

And this feeling did not deceive me, only at the time I did not guess that I myself would be the one to break the bond.

I know that my suffering in the following days was genuine and deep. And in thought I was living on with him.

I was giving tutorial lessons to little Olga at the time and often had to walk the long lovely Harvestehuder road there and back. I remember that I had conversations with him, as though he were walking beside me, so firmly had we grown together. And that went on all winter till Easter, with variations in temperature, naturally. The deep sincerity of my feeling for him developed at this time so that I said to myself: I shall always love him just as much, even though someday we are outwardly separated.

My friendship with Martha falls in that winter too. I had come to love this girl passionately and saw something higher in her, something better. I often went to her in the evening, clandestinely, of course, and felt at home and happy with her. I have often asked myself since how this crush of mine could ever have sprung up. For one thing, it was probably the novelty that charmed me. One felt about her the breath of that intellectual world Rolf had made dear to me. I admired her because she had raised herself above the sphere of interests of her social class. I could talk with her about Rolf. And finally, one point I had overlooked in my love at that time: her capacity to place her own good sides in a clear light, so that, being not too critical, one could easily see in her someone of a higher sort.

I was very worried about Rolf. In his pride he didn't want to accept any money from his father. Frau Pennarini, to be sure, was willing to teach him for nothing, only in return he was to tutor her little son in some school subjects. His funds were sufficient for only a short time. He kept looking more and more eagerly, and at last probably quite desperately, for a job. In the end he found one in a shop. He had to work there from 8 to 12 and from 2 to 8, then at noon to give the little Pennarini his lessons, and evenings to practice, take lessons, attend concerts and operas. This enormous burden of work for his delicate constitution. But when I once advised him to accept some money, he reproached me indignantly for having written that letter so thoughtlessly. I racked my brains for days on end thinking how I could provide money for him. But the money I got for lessons I had to give to Mother, and how could I earn anything worthwhile in addition?

I have often asked myself how I would have set up my life if he had not gone away that time. I now incline to the view that my life would have been chained fast to his—

and my love-life, which now has a ragged character, would have remained whole. Then the maternal quality in my love would have developed more vigorously, and it would not have become a stirring, flaming—but a peaceful, quiet happiness or at least a kind of happiness.

But it is idle thought to ask oneself questions like these. Yet on the other hand I cannot understand how such an incident as Rolf's departure in the end really was or could be decisive for my life. For I am convinced: if he had stayed I would have remained faithful to him. But in his long absence my senses did at last awaken—I yielded to them—and, as recompense, they took Rolf.

I believe this is the only occasion in my life about which I have said to myself: had I only known!! Had I not been so blind then, so irresponsibly blind!

Naturally the whole complicated process of disintegration cannot simply be understood with this one formula—but I believe that it is the *leitmotif*.

It began with a period I then designated the most peaceful, "happiest" of my life—the period of rehearsals and performance for Ernst's graduation.

At the rehearsals we were always exuberant—we played tag around the old wings of the Wandsbeck town theater, we recited Horace, we danced for hours. I had many small admirers among the players, and since I was not used to that I liked it immensely. An actor from the German Theater coached us, a Herr Matthaes. He was fat and homely, his acting was elegant and clever—but I'm digressing too far—the point is this, that as a man he exerted a charm on me stronger than I had ever felt. It was at the dress rehearsals. We wore Greek costumes and loose hair. When I was through with my part I went to sit in the proscenium box to watch. Presently M. came and joined me, remained silently sitting beside me and apparently didn't dare come closer—and went away again. My blood was boiling so that I was scarcely clear in the head. Afterward we talked together in the corridor—when he suddenly pulled me into the box and kissed me—kissed me. I climbed the narrow stairway that led to our dressing-room in a feverish glow.

The performance next day and the ball brought me many harmless pleasures, much homage that made me happy. My passion for the fat M. was soon over. When it threatened to become too strong I went to him, and that sobered me. But it had a critical effect on my relationship to Rolf. I had confessed to him the dress rehearsal incident because I felt I owed it to him. But he rejected my self-accusation on the grounds that he had no right to reproach me on that account. I had not expected such a mild judgment from Rolf —it brought me to the point of deceiving him from now on without any qualms of conscience. In May I had managed to meet him for a day—he had meanwhile come to Berlin. I wept with joy on seeing him again. We went to the woods together, we ate lunch in a solitary inn—he went to the piano and sang—it was strange: no song would come to our minds but "Days of the Roses." So he sang it 3 or 4 times. Then we went into the empty dance hall and danced about with joy. It was a scorchingly hot day—when we came to a little stream we swam, he in one corner, I in another. And then we went slowly back to the train. I enjoyed the day enormously—but it was too short for Rolf to have been able to bind me to himself again.

In the middle of July I went off to Switzerland with Selma, and shook off the dust and the dirt. It was in Chamonix one evening that I went into the mountains alone. It was already nearly dark, only from time to time a flash of lightning lit up the region. Thunder growled in the distance. I walked quickly ahead, almost as though I had an objective—but I was only escaping from Selma's mindless company. All around me Nature, grand, sublime— I felt utterly lonely and deserted. So that I clung to the one person who loved me, to Rolf. And a deep oppressive longing seized me. I felt protected in the thought of him. I sensed the unbreakable bond embracing us. I saw that

only with him did I feel at home, at home only in his soul.
I softly recited Goethe's poem to myself:

Why did you implant in us deep insight,
Ah, you were in some past generation
Either sister or my wedded wife.*

Not as if at that moment I would have believed in a trans-
migration of souls—but for me it was the poetic expression
for the feeling of belonging to Rolf.

When I got home I sat down and wrote to him and spoke
of the feelings the lonely path in the Chamonix valley had
awakened in me.

Begged him to write to me soon. Now came an odd, ca-
lamitous mistake with his letters—perhaps it was meant to
be that way. In Basel I got a letter cast in a light, chatty
tone. It was no answer to my letter—but I didn't know that.
This letter, the tone of which hurt me, cooled down my
warm feelings for him considerably (I asked myself bitterly
why he said nothing about my letter) and in the meantime
a glowing love letter had arrived in Chamonix for me—
but I knew nothing of its existence. If I had received it at
the time, perhaps I would not have nourished the unhappy
passion that was to take Rolf from me—perhaps—

I could now despair over the chain of events, every
single one of which looked as though its purpose were to
separate me from Rolf. *Were they all chance?* Was it a
chance that just on my return home—a week before I
was to see Rolf again—I met Ernst? That we made that
tour through the heath together and slept in the haystack?
He kissed me that time, and the passions so fickle in the
beginning deepened so much in a few days that I thought
I could not do without him.

---

* Translation from Edwin H. Zeydel, *Goethe the Lyrist* (Chapel
Hill, N.C.: University of North Carolina Press, 1959). [Ed.]

I will try to do justice to my feeling for Ernst too, and not diminish it in Rolf's favor through subsequent bitterness. I loved Ernst—a simple, strong, elemental feeling, about which I need say no more. And he loved me too. In many things in us there ruled a remarkable agreement. He often expressed a thought I had, in the same form, the same picture. We had many little characteristics in common. And above all our personalities were essentially the same: dominant and well-developed intellectual life and alongside it a fairly deep emotional life. Then another thing: a similar mixture of naughtiness and usefulness or, let us say, of a tendency to an ordered life and bohemianism. He too had strong moods. We often sat together and he read Jacobsen to me; I almost think we both had a corresponding understanding of him. Everything in me rejoiced: this is the man I have been looking for, the man who is right for me and only me and I for him. I often lay awake in bed transfigured by the bliss of a wishless happiness.

On Wednesday evening of the following week I went to Berlin with Selma. I had first had to fight with mother for permission to make the trip. She didn't want me to go on Rolf's account. If that isn't bitter irony! I was to meet Rolf the next morning; by some misunderstanding we spent an hour and a half looking for each other. And that in the full blaze of the August sun. At last we met. I was annoyed with him because he was responsible for the last part of the unnecessary waiting. So we were both out of humor in the beginning, I with him, and consequently he with me. I told him all sorts of things about myself, among others also about Ernst. At that he suddenly said: "You're in love with him." Jealousy had probably sharpened his usual sensitivity. Driven into a corner, I explained to him that I was not certain about it myself, which was true at the time. Then he said almost tonelessly: "Then it's all over between us." I was paralyzed with fright at this totally unexpected statement of Rolf's. —Over, between Rolf and me!

That was something I just couldn't grasp. When at last I had understood that he really meant it in earnest, I began to sob as though my heart would break. I told him that I did so sincerely love him and could never, never do without him and that my feeling for the other man was still so uncertain—we must have set ourselves at rest on this point, for I remember we went around quite happily that afternoon to different cafés and to the Wertheim department store, to end up in the zoological gardens not meeting Selma in spite of our appointment—then we had supper together, sauntered around and in the process met Selma on Friedrichstrasse. We went into a café together, Rolf became more and more silent and finally impolite, which I attributed to his being tired.

The next morning he told me that he had reacted to my coldness. We went to the Grunewald together and there took a walk in the dreary solitude of the woods. We tormented each other. We talked of what concerned us most—and could come to no agreement. He did not want to wait till my feelings had clarified, he wanted my declaration that I loved him, "loved" not just "was fond of" him. And this I *could* not give him. We then came to talk of other general questions—but a streak of nervous irritation entered into the discussion. Each of us felt irritated, hurt, when the other stuck to his opinions—in the end the tears kept running down my cheeks. As we returned to the Grunewald station I actually had the conviction that it must be all over between us. I sat in the train and heedlessly picked at the glorious yellow roses he had given me. That irritated him still more, for, as he explained later, he had taken it as a symbolic action. We had both grown nervous, incapable of pursuing deeper feelings or ideas any further. And in this apathetic state we got out at the zoo in order to go to the city. Having got hungry meantime, we went into a zoo restaurant, sat down in the garden, and ate. It occurred to me that it would suit the mood to drink champagne. So we drank; full of defiance we toasted parting or staying together. Then we took a carriage and drove to his place. I asked him if I could make myself useful, as I didn't know what I was there for. He gave me a dreadfully torn jacket to mend. I mended in silence. He lay on the sofa. Then he suddenly begged me to stop sewing. As I didn't do so immediately, he ordered me to, irritated. I did as he wanted. And then I was to sit beside him. Really close. And to kiss him—more and more. —We were heated by the wine, it had robbed us of our cool deliberation and self-control. So I conceded to everything he wanted to hear. I needed someone to support and guide me, should he be that person? Yes, certainly, only he. Did I love him? Yes, I loved him. Him only? Him only.

His passion knew no bounds any more. And I no longer had myself under control. —I let him do what he wanted. After a while he suddenly became thoughtful and asked me whether he should desist; I just nodded.

Then we gradually quieted down, straightened our clothes, which was very necessary, and left, going into various cafés and to the hotel, for our train was to go at 6 o'clock. Rolf and Selma both begged me to take a later train, but I didn't waver for a moment: Ernst had promised to fetch us. Every moral concept must have been lacking in me at that moment. How was that possible!

If I offer as an excuse that I was so steeped in my love for Ernst, the question surely comes up why did I take so much pleasure in Rolf's love? And yet there is probably something true in it: I loved Ernst, honestly and deeply, but I was not yet fully conscious of this love myself.

But I was *conscious* of loving Rolf. Add to this, too, that in those days a kiss had no importance at all for me, then also that Rolf and I had kissed before, and that in consequence I didn't think much about it. I don't want to attempt any justification with this explanation. The immorality of my way of acting lay first in lack of *self-control* and above all in the fact that I was not acting *consciously*.

How the break then came I have already written down

(27 November 1905). This break was, of course, just the necessary sequel. Naturally, I was already completely under the spell of my love—I *had to* rebuff Rolf. Necessary sequel?? Well—the way *all* happening is necessary. But how if Rolf could have waited? Then we would not have separated again. Perhaps my life would then have grown richer, for the time of my "love" for Rolf is still my—I almost want to say, "holiest memory." I will cite briefly the few facts from the keystone, just for the sake of completeness:

In the middle of August I got a moving letter from him, begging: Love me *wholly* and be true to me. I wrote him that I could not promise him that since I loved Ernst, but that he would always and always be dear to me. He never answered that letter.

Almost simultaneously with this last exchange of letters came my break with Ernst. A series of insignificant misunderstandings brought me in my impetuous passion to the point of breaking with him totally.

So I was alone and had leisure to think. I longed for both of them and wavered back and forth between them in my feelings. In the end the longing for Rolf prevailed. I wrote him a long letter. But I did so on a false assumption, namely that Rolf's feelings for me were as unaltered as mine for him.

I could have foreseen that this was not the case. Rolf is indeed capable of very deep sympathies—but if this feeling is wounded, it does not heal again; he is unable outside his own line of thought to understand and respect motives that are foreign to him. Therefore he tears this feeling right out of his heart—and there remains an emptiness, not even a feeling of piety toward what was once sacred.

So he was done with me—wrote me so—and at the same time announced a visit to Hamburg. It must have been in December; I saw him twice in Hamburg. We went for a walk together. Those two days were bitter for me. He let me feel that I was nothing to him any more.

Since then I have not seen him again. When I came back from my first semester in Freiburg I went to see him in Berlin—he was away. He later wrote me a short cool letter of regret, and I answered once more, explaining why I had tried to see him—i.e., I don't believe I told him the deepest reason for it—that I loved him just as much as before.

That's all. What I hope for the future is this: I wish to be able to do him some kindness once more, to help him, to recompense him for what he was to me, and to atone for what I did to him.

Freiburg, 26 June 1907

It cannot be so long ago that I wrote down those "closing words." And already everything is changed. On the 24th June I got a kind letter from Rolf. He offers me his friendship again, referring to the words in my letter of August 1905, the closing words of that letter: "We both want from each other the conviction that we love each other *steadfastly*, etc." I was beside myself with joy. I went down on my knees, driven by the need to thank someone for this happiness. I read the letter again and again. And even today, after 2 days, I cannot yet grasp the fact that my most ardent wish has been fulfilled. I am waiting almost anxiously for a second letter from him in order to see that this first one was really no deception, no delusion.

Letters

to Oskar Horney,

1906–1907

OSKAR HORNEY

〜〜〜〜〜〜〜〜〜〜〜〜〜〜〜〜〜〜〜〜〜〜〜〜〜〜〜〜〜〜〜〜〜〜〜〜〜〜〜

Freiburg, 26 July 1906

[POSTCARD]

Dearly beloved sweet Hornvieh, our longing for you has grown to oo—$(a + b)^2 = a^2 + 2\,ab + b^2$. While it was raining so yesterday. Tomorrow, Thursday, you will on pain of death be at the Martinstor at 8:30 for the musical evening. $b_{18}H_{36} + o_{52} = 18\,b + 18\,H_2O$. In return for which we will come to you *Friday evening*. Du er en torsk.* Farewell, my precious brother in the Lord (Where?).

Karen Danielsen, stud. med.

---

* Presumably Karen's Danish for "you are a blockhead." The name Hornvieh, German for horned cattle—for which English has no singular—is also a term for a stupid person, a blockhead. One takes it as a play on the patronymic of Oskar Horney, from all accounts a rather brilliant man with a good mind, and as an ironic, affectionate nickname—untranslatable. [Ed.]

Fallingbostel, 4 September 1906

[POSTCARD]

Beloved Hornvieh, do let us hear from you for once, old fellow! Can't you come here for a bit? Losch is here too. —I would so frightfully like to hear you laugh again. And to philosophize with you, with Losch one just can't talk sense, as you know. . . . Now we are going out rowing with lanterns. And anyway it's ideal here. Write at least, do you hear? Hearty greeting and kiss from your

Karen

I've heard so much about you and your laughter. Come along with it!

— ? ! ! Losch

Döse near Cuxhaven, 10 September 1906

My dear little Hornvieh,

You think I'm still lying on the heath and dreaming, that it's going on and on like that with heather and juniper bushes into infinite distances—but see, my beloved brother in Christo, I'm already sitting enthroned high up on a pair of weathered stone veterans on the p[raemissis] p[raemittendis] North Sea and letting the sea wind mess up my hair and the surf spray foam in my face. And I am perfectly content with this change of scene.

> In the first place since one now and then
> can take a sea-bath here again.

(Please to properly admire my poetic vein!)
2. because of the crabs, and 3. the heath *is* wonderful and sympathetic to the remotest corner of my soul, *but* I feel more at home by the sea, more in my element. And that dear little Hornvieh has risen to writing whole epistles! I was much touched, and so was the *"really quite* dear fellow."

So I am to expatiate in detail on the possibilities of meeting? At first I wanted to write you a letter with all the advantages of that little nest, that divine Fallingbostel and Braunschweig. But I thought that even with your philosopher's peace you would not have managed it, so I let it be. Furthermore I suggest that we three meet ca. October 15th in Hannover. Yes? I look forward terribly to seeing you again and above all to listening to you—God, what beautiful hours those were on your balcony in Günthersthal! Do you remember?—when you explained to me how you had come to an understanding with those various big question marks. You know, I have found so few people with whom I could have conversed about deeper-lying things, and therefore I am the less likely to forget those hours.

Have you really read a great deal? I mean, philosophical things. I find all systematic philosophical writing tiresomely difficult and incomprehensible. Perhaps you will publish one too, when your messy rubbish is finished. Then I will read it—i.e., *not* the fecal matter. *That* you can't ask of me. So, and now I will go swimming. The waves are running high —and that is still better than philosophy!

For the rest, I go to Geestemünde Friday, Dockstrasse for a week and, to close with a fine phrase, "will always be glad to hear from you."

Affectionately, your Karen

Geestemünde, Dockstrasse, 18 September 1906

Dear little Hornvieh,

So you're the first to get a sensible letter from here—"sensible," that is, in contrast to various birthday-thanks epistles (my dear, I am now 21!!, haven't you a frightful amount of respect for me?)—well, then, epistles mainly for a skull that in future will be the ornament of my room. Whether this letter will turn out sensible? I doubt it. For I feel not quite fresh, and in consequence sluggish in thinking and feeling. Should not this intensive influence by something purely physical on my whole way of thinking really cease the moment I become conscious: that you now incline to splash through life in heavy rubber boots is due only to your physical fatigue!? I find it absurd—and yet I bow under the yoke. *A propos* thinking, "one's own thinking"! Whether I—?? Yes, unremitting, ever more refined self-observation that never leaves me, even in any sort of intoxiation—then, if I have butted up against some problem, i.e., if I am myself sitting in the puddle, then I gather some "thoughts" together until I am in the clear with the affair; these are so-to-speak practical problems, religious conflicts—friendship-love—love-marriage—sense and nonsense of the demands of convention. But there are countless others, aren't there, that fumble around at the border of consciousness—and whether I can develop any so-called thinking of my own among such abstract problems, I do not know. No, absolutely not. At most, so that I can understand how they are meant. In any case I shall get at this Lange when I have finished Weismann (*Theory of Descent*), which in fact fascinates me *enormously*. —Your exuberant verbiage dangerous? So far as I'm concerned you can write 37 pages on the appropriate succession of pages in a letter or any other such blameless theme, you old pedant, you—I love so to listen when you talk with me. And that brings

[166]

to mind that I wanted to ask you something else, that time, but then your boozing got in the way. Remember, we were once talking about freedom of the will—and you told finally how you had come to some conclusion about the question of responsibility. And I was so tired that evening, and it didn't penetrate into my brain. Will you tell me again? Losch has probably written you meanwhile? His address is Hildesheim, Gartenstr. 39. He is a *dear*. Under his cheekiness there is something pure, childlike, it is the artist in him. And that indestructible freshness—on the heath we naturally romped around like two young dogs. O God, little Hornvieh, I am now in such a petit-bourgeois atmosphere of *"respectability"* [in English], young-lady manners, maid-servants—and talk about clothes—oh, I naturally move around in this milieu appropriately and converse exhaustively about whether Hirschfeld or Feldberg makes better suits. In the long run such an atmosphere always makes me restless, to the point of turning somersaults and the like—indeed it does. So my dear little Hornvieh—now I'm going to sleep. The *matchiche* melody keeps running through my mind.

cette danse, qui nous agiche
c'est la Matchiche—

—well, good night
your Karen

Hamburg, Hallerstr. 61, 6 October 1906

My dear little Hornvieh,
To take essentials first: about meeting—well, it will probably come to nothing. I will explain the reasons with

my boring thoroughness. 1) Losch doesn't go till the 20th, whereas I go the 15th. 2) Said "I" of preceding sentence is not going alone but with her girl-friend. Same, however, will go straight through.

Voilà. My soul is mortally dejected. *Mais que faire?* Turn round and round on your heels and think the world has gone dizzy—

So now you old pedant will get angry again over the nevertheless perfectly sensible sequence of my writing-paper pages, eh? The *little* Hornvieh!

Just think, my dear, Losch will live with us too!! What do you think of that? It has its two sides, doesn't it? But now on the heath we have become much closer and are, I believe, on the way to becoming a pair of good comrades. Perhaps it will happen. We also have just about the same work—that is probably a factor not to be underestimated. So. . . .

I was on the heath again yesterday. With a boy-friend of my youth. Lord, how cutely patriarchal that sounds! We went right through the brown heather, it reached to our knees. And we lay there for hours, letting the warm October sun work an infinite well-being into all our limbs. Talked hardly at all—though some verses of Storm came to my lips. That was a day. A few well-sounding verses can mean a great deal to me, I can often repeat them over and over to myself.

Today to the Ohlsdorf cemetery. The dead have it good there: rose-hedges, birch-groves, dusky paths under pines, little ponds with water lillies framed in wonderful groups of trees and plants, etc. And the colors now—incredible.

I write you only about enjoying—but my life is now just *one* enjoyment. Now? No, really always. It is as though everything has turned into enjoyment in my hands. Perhaps because everything I do—or almost everything—I attack intensively. Whether learning chemical formulas or making a pudding or reading something beautiful or being out in the open—profligate epicure, eh? Except when a

couple of those sluggish days come along—then everything goes askew. Brrr! Then I slip out of my own hands.

I catch myself from time to time inquiring whether our
ethical demands, in our emotional life at least, do not turn
out to be simply the demand for the greatest possible enjoyment!? I'll give you a perfectly banal example: if I kiss
a man out of love, I undoubtedly get greater pleasure from
it than when I do so instinctively, from some sort of
bubbling over. The first is at the same time ethically higher.
—But perhaps this is just a playing with words. —I'm just
writing away, whatever comes into my head, hardly
realizing that someone else is to read it. Little Hornvieh
functionings as Karen's diary! I am often confused by there
being such a plethora of fundamentally different people.
There is my little girl-friend here, the one who is going with
me, you know: enchantingly graceful and coquettish, one of
those conscious coquettes who is fully aware of every little
charm, loyal to herself and to me in the subtlest ways,
utterly lazy, very touchy, and as she admits herself, quite
cowardly, frivolous—and the whole mixture *perfect* in its
own way, and there is a great charm in it too.

My brother an extremely sharp-thinking intellectual, cool
skeptic and cynic.

My father a big child, whose world of ideas revolves
around a strong, touchingly naïve belief in the Bible.

And each of them of course considers only his own
character as justified, only his own glasses through which
he looks at the world!

I believe there are only two things that can enrage me
with people: plain, satiated philistinism and intrinsic mendacity.

These thoughts are whirling around in my head. Writing
is, of course, so clumsy and burdensome!

And then the *Tannhäuser* music of night before last
rings in my head—the Venus music in the Overture—I had
to think of *Tristan*: "and then came that ascent of the
violins, which is higher than all reason." Higher than all

reason—yes, it is breath-taking, oppressive, I want to scream. I can hardly wait for Losch to play for me again.

Today I heard the following: a married man loves a girl ("loves" used in its deepest meaning). He does not regret that he has married someone else, but says: she was what I needed *at that time*. Isn't that a most profound reason against marriage? Against its indissolubility? But the children! *Je ne sais pas.*

No, my dear, I really must stop. I think I have treated you to an infinite amount of mixed-up chatter. Mother wrote from Freiburg today, especially enthusiastic about Günthersthal, and she had already discovered the balcony of the Hornvieh from our map and I had been a frightfully dissipated rascal in those days. But for these, just these last 2 weeks I would gladly give up all the rest of the semester. Amen.

So long! I find it incredible, my dear, that you acquired such an unqualifiable (Mercy, how hard to write!) name as "Oskar." But for me you have another name.

I greet you

Karen

Hamburg, 12 October 1906

[POSTCARD]

Little Hornvieh,

Do you really think then, stupid, that I would have written you if I had not *beforehand* broken my head thinking out the possibilities? My friend is *only* allowed to come along under my motherly guidance, we are being sent off together by her parents—so there! I think you know yourself that I would love to do it—and find it *bad* of you to reproach me for lack of desire and initiative. Yes, sir. We will postpone our meeting till Freiburg then? But you must not be angry at me for this, do you hear? On the contrary, you ought to console me! But in your egoism that naturally doesn't occur to you. *O me miseram!* You dung beetle! A whole love-letter on a picture postcard!

Vale!

Karen

Freiburg, 19 October 1906

Herewith I announce to your Reverence that I have arrived safe and sound in body and soul in Freiburg and have opened my domicile at Sedanstr. 12, *que je serais inconsolable si vous étiez fâché, que je serais très heureuse* to hear the contrary or to hear from you anyway.

Je vous embrasse mille fois, mon ami

Karen

Freiburg, Sedanstr. 12, some day in November 1906

Hornvieh, little one, dear one,

Enfin seule—I could cry out with pathos. For Losch and Idchen are at the Rheingold. Otherwise we are usually together evenings, either in the way of taking a walk, or Losch plays—or we read aloud, or we work, or we have visitors, or we fool around (oh!) But it is always inexpressibly cozy. For Mother is here and she knows not only how to cook well, but above all how to spread about her a

fluid atmosphere of coziness. And then our living room!
When one first comes in, one thinks one has always lived
in it. It is like that. And then we four are all so fond of one
another, each individual of each individual. So that the
thought of our home has something infinitely calming, so
that one is happy when one comes home after a lecture. I
missed that so much, this—how to say it—this atmosphere
of tenderness about me. Big people are supposed to be able
to be alone, I can't do it without suffering from it. I mean
external solitude.

Inwardly—it probably lies in the nature of the case that
one is always alone there, and yet moments when one becomes conscious of this are so painful. At least for me.

"Become conscious of," how lightly one passes it over in
writing! And still cannot grasp what it means. —Today for
the first time skipped a lecture. Wiedersheim was demon-
strating an abdominal situs and rummaged around vol-
uptuously in the intestines. I bore it very bravely. Yes,
really! Nevertheless we preferred to go to the café and then
up the Schlossberg. It was fine. Below, fog thick enough
to cut. Above, ice-clear. And he is such a dear, Losch!

We were recently on the Schauinsland mountain top and
once in the St. Valentin valley. As we came past little Hornvieh's balcony we whistled. But—

Hurry up and finish your dirty business, my dear! You
can't be held responsible anyway for science and agriculture
waiting so long! How selfless I am, am I not?

Whether she is really my friend? Yes. I am very fond of
her. What makes her valuable to me is above all her being
honest with herself—so few people are that. And I find that
whatever a person always does or is, he is sympathetic to
me if he does it consciously. I believe you said once consciousness = morality. That I don't understand. For if, for
example, my brother acts in every event with full, keen
consciousness on the principle of carefully weighed interest,
that surely is not "moral" for that reason! Or is it? Perhaps

the concept "morality" unconsciously combines for me with selflessness, with an antithesis to Nature and instinct. Rudiments perhaps of my Christian period.

Well, now I've got off the subject of Idchen. Yes, she is studying, and both German and history, tells everyone she works from noon till 1 and evenings until 7. (She does begin around 12, and around 5!) She is awfully cunning. Well, you'll get to know her.

Tomorrow Losch and I begin dissection. At first I was terribly afraid of the dissecting room, but that is gone now and I look forward to the work. Losch and I have the same preparation to do on the same body, so we can work well together. He is frightfully industrious now and unusually steady.

The question of going home for Christmas is pretty well solved, because my "home" is now here. In Hamburg there is only my father. And I have no contact with him. I will get myself the Nietzsche volume soon.

12 November 1906

I think it is more than a week that this letter has been lying here, begun. I have been solemnly proclaiming to Losch every day: today I really want to write to our little Hornvieh. But—

For a few days we were in the dissecting room for hours —and furthermore I am thrilled to be there. It goes horribly well. Only you don't get rid of the smell—oh well, on Friday, we finished with the neck muscles, and then we two went up on the Solacker after dinner! The same steep path as in those days when we stuck a blade of grass ½ cm long into little Hornvieh's nose—. Then Kybfelsen. And at sunset! The sky was all dipped in a glow. So pitch black afterward that we lost our way a couple of times.

Sunday Feldberg. Saw the Alps. God, how beautiful it is here. Hurry up, my dear! And then again a day of most intensive work like today, so that afterward a feeling of blessed weariness comes over you, almost like a slight champagne tipsiness. And then I lie on the sofa all hidden in pillows and blankets—and Losch plays a Chopin prelude.

Losch and I—I had almost been afraid we would get "fed up" with each other living together; but the bond has only become firmer, more solid through it. I could write pages about our relation to each other, and I would also like to put down some things that are in my heart. But a certain shyness keeps me from talking to you about it. I feel that would be unfair to Losch. So no more of that. Little Horn-vieh is of course an expert in this field too—yet every new, shall we say, "love" brings a new world with it.

There's still such chaos in me. Still so little firmly outlined. Just like my face: a formless mass that only takes on shape through the expression of the moment. The searching for our selves is the most agonizing, isn't it?—and yet the most stimulating—and one simply cannot escape it. And when once again one stands helpless: what are you? In school we always had to trace a character from a fundamental characteristic. I involutarily try that in life too. But most of the time I fail. And perhaps it's nonsense.

. . . I hardly get to any reading now. To work from 6 to 8 with one hour break. Then one is tired. . . . Christmas! I've been running around after the article in the review. . . . I'll go flirt a little with one assistant professor of anatomy and try to pump it out of him. I can't tell you how happy I am to be studying medicine. How did you ever get into jurisprudence? Do tell me a little about yourself! Will you? I am already *looking forward* to a letter from you. Yes. *Very much.*

But now goodnight!

Your Karen

Freiburg, Sedanstr. 12, 11 December 1906

My little Hornvieh,

At noon today Losch came home with the happy message that we shall have a new corpse on Thursday. You know, that is such real work, it gives me tremendous joy. Then I thought I would quickly make use of this free day to write to my Hornvieh-friend.

It is actually 3 weeks already since your last letter. As I write this, the evening rises vividly before me again. We came home overtired from the dissecting room. Your letter was lying on the table. We sat down—and I began to read the first sentences aloud. Then I got stuck and read it to myself. Yes, and then—don't laugh, please!—then I was suddenly lying there on our sofa, my head hidden in the pillows and something hot came into my eyes. You can well imagine Losch's astonishment—and at the time I couldn't account for it myself—I was not at all clear why such a desperate sadness overcame me. Then I naturally began racking my brains, till I found a satisfactory explanation. —As I write, I am afraid of writing about it, and making the reservation that I will not send the letter. Whew, bad! If I didn't even want to—or couldn't!—be honest with little Hornvieh! How do you manage to make me feel ashamed of playing tricks on you? I believe, because you are yourself so true and because you can understand and because you are good. Thus the pious Catholic goes to the priest for confession. But you are not a priest, you are a human being.

But I wanted to tell you about what your letter awakened in me.

Look—a good 2 years ago something decisive entered into my life in the form of a languishing Jewish youth. That smacks of a "great love," etc.—but—he showed me, who had only breathed the air of a petit-bourgeois family, a life of a higher sort. I came into a whole circle of young people who were all honestly seeking truth in knowledge and morality and *acted* accordingly. That lasted perhaps a year. It was an infinitely meaningful friendship that brought us both a deep, pure happiness. Well, and then out of the blue I was seized by a senseless passion for someone else, who was built of a coarser stuff. I loved my little friend none the less on that account—there simply are feelings that lie so deep they are untouched by all personal vicissitudes, isn't that so?—but that he couldn't understand. Also he couldn't wait. I had to choose. So I gave him up.

For a long time I did not know what I had given up with him.

I managed to adapt myself again imperceptibly to the coarser way of thinking of my surroundings.

And now your letter. That was the finer language again, which extends beyond workaday jargon—you understand? The tone struck me—the whole period after that break had seemed to me so unspeakably useless and grey. Not that I yearned for the person of my little friend—I believe it was grief, rather, that I had slipped down like that from the level of those days.

Now you see what you have done. Cast a glaring spotlight. —But grieving over times past is useless. One can then only conjure up how everything had to happen as it did, just as it did. Belief in the necessary in life calms me. So isn't it silly when, nevertheless, self-reproaches now and again creep in? But *why* do they come *anyhow*?

What is Losch to me? Perhaps I can be something to him.

When I read in Nietzsche's aphorisms the one "about the generosity of women" I had to think of our relationship. But again it doesn't fit. I am too young for that. Perhaps it is this that makes him so fond of me. It brings to mind a passage from *Zarathustra*: "The honor of woman is: to love more than she is loved. Hence prostitution begins here," or something of the sort. There is surely some truth in it, but like all aphorisms, one-sided. You put a question mark after the expression "Woman's Friendship." Nietzsche here approximates Weininger's explanation. I once read: a man and a woman can only sustain friendship if both carry love for others in their hearts. But one really can't get at a problem of this sort with such short sentences. If one understood "love" the way the wonderful Greek story pictures it, how human beings were halved at the Creation and now everyone seeks his complementary half, then of course there would be only one love for every person and everything else would be put on the market under the trademark "Friendship." Or "Experiments in Love," "Liebesversuche," as in Renate Fuchs. Do you know the book? I am very fond of it. Its effectiveness probably springs only from the fact that one required of such a "friendship between man and woman" absolute unsensuousness, drawing an artificial line between love and friendship. If one lets that drop, to my mind the problem as such falls away anyhow.

The part about a "protean nature" applies only to certain unindividual women, in that context at least I think very highly of men who can bear to love a woman just as she is without demanding that she be in one certain uniform. "From the Future of Marriage"—I couldn't endure it, I believe, to share a man I truly loved, even with only a prostitute. You yourself write about exclusivity in marriage. What you told me about your girl-friend moved me deeply. Do you really think then that the need, the demand for exclusivity is an instinctive drive of a lower order that a higher civilization can overcome? But that conquest must be an endless torment!

I am infinitely sympathetic with your shying off big words. People who present you with highly stilted words on a silver platter awaken an instinctive mistrust in me. One simply *cannot* speak of what occupies one most deeply, most burningly. A thing that I like in Weininger, e.g., "on the shamelessness of a declaration of love." Have you read Weininger? I am at it again, as you have probably noticed. The man impresses me frightfully in part and I am looking for points of attack. He confuses me at the moment because he brings forward so many really plausible observations in support of his thesis. But it cannot, must not, may not be like that.

So, but now I have to think of closing off. Saturday and Sunday, Feldberg with skis. Nine hours to get up there. Danced in the evening. Oh Hornvieh, were those the days! How lovely to be young.

Next week Losch and Idchen go away. Sonni and I probably to Switzerland or somewhere. Our home is often like a doll's house:

Sonni – the stepmother
Losch – the husband
Karen – the wife
Idchen – their daughter

A tantalizing little idyl. A lot of dear people. The little girl really delightful, with half Freiburg so far as concerns masc. gen. at her feet. So—and *when are you coming*? When will we be able to stop having to think immediately of our little Hornvieh at every manure pile?

Skiing is divine! Come quick!

Greetings from all here.

Your Karen

27 December 1906

[WRITTEN FROM THE BLACK FOREST]

Hornvieh, dear one, little one,

You know, I am quite alone this evening. Sonni has faithlessly left me and gone back to Titisee. Well yes, to the Feldberg farm. And I seem to myself so helpless among all those strangers. Now I have fled to my room. So, now the Hornvieh has sat down beside me—you see I am no longer so disconsolate—now we will have a chat. And what would we be talking about if you were really here? I try to imagine how you look—but I only remember that from time to time your unruly *"forelocks"* [in English] fell over your brow and that always looked so tremendously funny. Pff, didn't it though? I don't even remember whether you are big or small, and have gone so far as to quarrel with Losch on that account; I thought you were quite small and he laughed at me. That probably comes from the "little" Hornvieh, about which a longer lecture in well chosen words on the association of ideas is superfluous. Oh, what a cultured sentence! Superfluous! But my dear Karen, I believe you lack true seriousness and dignity! You are writing to the Hornvieh! Yes, but I may prattle about things like this with the little Hornvieh, mayn't I? If only you were sitting here, you would certainly laugh at my having so much respect for you. Oh, well. I do still remember how you laugh. That just gives me a smart idea: haven't you a human picture of *yourself*? *For* me? Look, I really haven't any of me, otherwise I would gladly have sent you 3 or 4. I'm always bad on properly taken photos. A certain expression always comes out (forced of course) which afterward appears quite absurd. You would have to snap me 50 times in succession and present the thing as a movie—then. Whereas—well, etc. Moreover in your masculine naïveté you naturally think I have become still crazier in the matter of letter pages. But sometimes I have no blotter or the least thing that resembles one, and wait till the stuff is dry! The way one waits for the coffee water to boil. Not just now. Filled out the waiting time with tidbits. Offered you some too. Have become quite cheerful now. Just think, I had gone through a metamorphosis in the last 6 days, I had become an old professor with spectacles, a bald pate, and wrinkles, and studied from early morning to late evening and had no thought for anything but my work, not even for sweets! I have an embryo at home in alcohol, which we with parental pride call Idchen's youngest brother —well, I dissected the said embryo. Hornvieh, why aren't you an M.D.? It's a failure in your character! Indeed it is! Now *if* you were an M.D. I would expound to you with full particulars why I am ecstatic about this embryo. You are certainly thanking your Creator that you don't need to listen to that?! But joking aside: this intensive working has given me a deep, pure joy—I now understand the one sentence in your letter that was incomprehensible to me at first, where you spoke of a scholar in whom research had absorbed all sensuality. One feels oneself so free then from the material, supersensual. Sonni naturally saw the matter with concern—and I was at once transported hither. For Sonni operates with the word "healthy" a great deal. That is all well and good, but it involves a disregard of everything that goes beyond a certain borderline. But what then is it that makes us happy? In any case it is always something that goes beyond the ordinary measure. For example, I would find it crazy to be sitting here in this more or less cold room, chatting the evening away with my Hornvieh. But this way I am happy, whereas down there despite warmth, etc., I should feel very uncomfortable. Generally speaking: she is not free from the mistake, frequent enough, to be sure, of setting up a norm meant for everybody. "Only nothing too much!"—a little friendship, a little work, a little idling, etc. So, now I have just begun with what it is about her that I sometimes find hard to take. If, however, I give up requiring understanding in finer things, in what lies deeper, then she seems to me a truly perfect, exemplary mother. She is almost as serene and unworried as a child, and has not let herself be robbed of her gaiety through all the difficulties she lived through in her marriage. In her emotions too she is like a child, strong in hating and loving, not listening to reason. She is touchingly selfless. She is *not at all* petty. In short she is a person one *has to* love. So, there I am in the middle of telling about the doll's house. I want to go right on with it. But I am really beginning to freeze. Come along, Hornvieh, let's run up and down outside a couple of times.

So, here we are again. And now it is quite comfortable here. Whee, how cutting the cold was. The snow crunched under every step. Perfectly light. Moonlight. The big white flat areas were quite ghostly, and behind them the pine tree tops. It should be lovely to walk through the snow-covered woods now. Perhaps, no surely, down to the Feldsee. —But quite alone? Naa, much too timid.

But I wanted to tell you. Do Idchen and Losch irritate each other? No, *not at all*. They are awfully fond of each other. On the one hand they are both lovable—then Idchen is above all too passive, so that any disharmony would be uncomfortable for her. And Losch has little vanity. They are also alike in many things, e.g., they both have an instinctive aversion to philosophy and instead an immense realism. Idchen, for example, has a pronounced aversion to great emotions in general, e.g., sacrificing for the sake of an idea is incomprehensible and unsympathetic to her. But of course Losch has his music, in which he can lose himself. He has a rich emotional life anyway, he can suffer under an emotion (which is for me the criterion of the depth of a feeling). On the other hand Idchen has a really warm feeling, I believe, only for me, otherwise she plays with it—intelligence predominates. Where Losch is concerned there is also the fact that Idchen has a perfectly miraculous way of taking individual people—she draws their weaknesses right out and operates with them. But all this I am writing you about her she is fully *aware* of herself. And that reconciles me. One can't be angry with the delightful creature anyway, when one is with her—amusing, lively, and quite unusually graceful in mind and body. —So, but enough for today. Goodnight, little Hornvieh. And tomorrow evening you will come to me again, won't you? Only a pity that I have to bear the whole cost of the entertainment. I would of course much rather listen silently while you talked. Or read a letter from you.

28 December 1906

Good evening, little Hornvieh, here I am with you again. All my limbs are aching—I've been skiing all day, just a brief break for lunch. Hornvieh my dear, how I *love life!* A couple of verses by a Hamburg poetess occur to me. "I lived so long in the stifling valley/I went in torment mute so long/and had forgotten in all that suffering/that over the mountains in glory/the sun strides every morning." When you stand in the midst of all those heights so fresh with snow and look down into all the deep gorges around about and look over the pine forests all around that are so fabulous in their jewelry of frost—and over it all a triumphant red glow of dawn—far off on the horizon the long chain of proud immaculate Alpine peaks tinged by the first rays of the sun—my dear, my heart opens wide and instinctively I spread out my arms in reverence and joy at that magnificence. I keep timidly away from the people here. I cannot overcome this stupid shyness. In the company of people who are not close to me I often feel so remote and as though I don't belong.

Your letter—yes, now I will try not to be afraid of you any more. The thought that you want to be my friend makes me happy. You know that you can be, no, are a great deal to me now. And there again is your fate, of which you spoke in your first letter to me: to give to everyone more than is given to you. For what am I to you! Losch cannot help me there. What does he think of your letters? I have shown him practically nothing of the last ones, for I had the feeling they had been written for me alone. At first he was—jealous! Now I think he has understood that you are taking nothing from him, for what you are to me he cannot be at all. And yet he would rather have me entirely to himself. And if he wasn't fond of you too, he might be just as glad if you did not exist. I understand that perfectly well—but I can't change it.

Have just collected all my housewifely experiences and lit a fire, having been about to freeze. Little Hornvieh as good housewife. Ah children, I do mistrust the business! Do you prepare your own supper? And what sort of a fellow is your friend anyway? And when are you coming this way? I think I have asked that in every letter! Yes, indeed! But never got an answer!

So—now I will go to bed. I'll probably have to go down to Freiburg again tomorrow as there's no room here.

One thing more: I believe that the Jews with that fine-feeling sensitivity are a quite vanishing small number among their own race. But those few are for that reason particularly valuable people, and are so through their influence on others. For they are themselves for the most part too weak for the battle of life.

I have read the article. Will write about it next time. Then I will send it back to you. If you would send me the little book you spoke of, I would be grateful. You have cheered two dismal evenings for me with your company. And don't even know about it. Funny.

But now I'll really stop. No, must still thank you for your Christmas card!

Your Karen

13 January 1907

My dear little Hornvieh,

It suddenly weighs on my conscience that I haven't sent the journal back yet. Please forgive. And many thanks! The article naturally interested me very much. I tried at the time to give an account of it in a brief abstract. Unfortunately I haven't it at hand, but still I will try to say briefly what I think about it:

1)   He neglects the economic question too much. Conditions for earning one's living are more difficult now, hence girls *have* to take part in it too.

2)   I agree with R. in that I too doubt that women will *ever* be able to achieve intellectually what men do. Lies in the nature of the matter—women are too involved in the sexual—children! etc. So that the woman question won't bring any direct advance in the life of the mind (science, art).

3)   On the other hand I do *not* believe that the cultivation of emotional life, which according to R. is the woman's cultural task, will be restricted thereby. Comparison with Sparta is no help! He says, e.g., that the relation of the sexes to each other would be unfavorably altered by it. I think just the opposite is the case. Just compare the charming comradely relation between men and women students— and the unnatural formal intercourse between young people of different sex in the better social classes!

4)   "It is not the *learned* woman who can be something to the man as mother-friend-wife." No, certainly not *because* of her learning, because of her knowledge. It doubtless happens often enough *now still* that women are proud of their *knowledge*. The *exactly* corresponding comparison is the parvenu, who is proud of his money. But the *general level* of culture rises. Knowledge to my mind is something quite secondary—but women will begin to reflect, even if it only means at first that they grasp the phenomena of custom, religion, personality, etc., etc., *as problems*, and cease looking in a limited way on what is given as if it were sacred.

5)   That *eventually* the population increase would suffer (?) seems to me to signify no great danger, for it will *always* be only a small percentage of women who work at such a highly intellectual level that their capacity for

motherhood would suffer, and then after all it really does not depend on a few people more or less!

So, that's about it!

I was so very glad to get your letter. Now I can think myself so well into your way of life. And I'll pay you a visit soon too! Yes! At Easter. *If* I come up, certainly. I.e., naturally if little Hornvieh—pooh, how stupid—do you know what I was about to write?—"if little Hornvieh would like it too."

Yesterday Basel: enjoyed Böcklin—Holbein.

Have to work frightfully hard—generally from 8 to 8. Evenings we sew on our costumes of colored patches. We started out with the same material and the same purpose, and it is significant that Idchen's dress is turning into a beggar *princess* dress and mine more a gypsy dress.

So I don't get to much reflection. —Now I've just begged Losch with gentle force for his corpse picture. But you must return it! . . .

I have also continued writing on a piece of autobiography —about the time of spiritual awakening of course.

Does little Hornvieh keep a diary or something of the sort?

My dear, have you really no family any more, so that you were so alone—New Year's Eve, for example?

So, now I must go out front again.

So I'll stop.

I am looking forward again to a letter from you. —It often seems to me that I am living all the time in over-heated rooms here, as though I would suffocate under all the love and care surrounding me.

I greet you

Karen

Freiburg, 5 February 1907

Good day, Hornvieh, dear, here I am again. I feel as though I had not written you for a long, long time, and as though that had been a painful privation for me.

I know I have so often thought of writing you—and yet preferred to get off 10 letters first saying nothing to indifferent people. Probably that fear again of giving too much, of spiritual undressing—or perhaps because I have a dull suspicion that I could hardly manage to clothe in words what is oppressing me. But you are clever and good.

I have everything, everything, haven't I, that a person could ask in order to be happy—satisfying work, love, home, natural surroundings. etc.

And I take deep pleasure in enjoying everything that is offered. And yet the feeling comes creeping up more often than ever, what is all this for? You see, quite ordinary sophomoric *Weltschmerz*! And I, I'm almost ashamed to have it. It sounds so incredibly immature. I have to smile at it myself—and that doesn't get rid of it. Perhaps it comes from being all the time with only these dear big children, who can mean so miserably little to me now. Sometimes it seems to me I am freeing myself more and more from Losch, and yet he is so unspeakably dear and kind to me. But I often think: little Hornvieh lives much more alone than I—how do *you* manage not to get tired of living? Of this eternal useless sameness!

Ah, anyone who can have a child's faith, like my Father! "The good Lord wants it that way"—Pooh, it's really cowardly to long for such a thing. I'm even going to Rickert now.* If one is really looking for something, one also looks where there doesn't seem to be much prospect.

And at the same time I can dance nights through in self-forgetful joy.

---

* Presumably the English priest and poet Marcus Rickert (1840–1928). [Ed.]

Hornvieh, do help me—I believe I am wandering in a special labyrinth and shall never get out, and see only my own picture everywhere, but always so extremely different. I shall nevertheless go to Hamburg at Easter, merely to visit you. For otherwise? In Hamburg lounging around, theater, dancing, strange faces—all that stimulates me only from time to time, and then I can have it here too.

Now I have dreamed along beyond this letter—would rather write more another time—today it would only be confused stuff anyway.

9 February

I feel it is impudent to write you today. It is as though one went into the living room in dirty boots. And yet I would like to sit beside you now, quite quiet, eyes closed—and then peace would be in me too—little Hornvieh, you experienced reader of men's souls, have you got wind of what's behind it? *Lendemain* mood.

13 February

Today is Ash Wednesday—and I have come to the conclusion that probably not much is the matter with me. Still —perhaps I'm a genius at bumming around—there still is something. I've read what I wrote you on the 9th—that was the Free Students' Carnival Ball—oh yes, with lots of champagne.

It has gone on the same way since—and yesterday we were out late dancing in the Festhalle. And it was frightfully common there. The atmosphere stifling and heavy with wine fumes and kissing. Just look, and I didn't go again right away—it intoxicated me, infected me—and I was not better than all the others. And you must not think me better than I am—that's why I have to tell you all this. Perhaps there is a bit of the hussy in all of us. But then something like this gets me all confused again, don't know what to think of myself, whether I am really serious about my striving for knowledge, my striving to become something.

22 February

It seems this letter will never get off. But I am so longing for a letter from you—for a long letter. Tell me about yourself, tell whatever comes into your head—anything makes me happy that comes from you. I am not coming *now*. I am so tired. I look forward to their all being away, need badly to be alone with myself again. And then I will write you often—yes, may I? —You must be patient with me now. I think I have been utterly flattened out lately; a sultry feeling tells me so, the yawning emptiness in me and the disgust. I *believe* I *could* amount to something pretty good. But not like this; this way I'm going backward. I now understand the one drive in monasticism—the pathos of distance—not making oneself common with others—

> never give in to mediocrity;
> once you have got on with it
> you soon will be at flat as it is!

Hornvieh, write me now—so that I have someone once more to whom I can look *up*.

If you would come now!

Farewell
your Karen

Freiburg, 24 March 1907

My little Hornvieh,

Oh pooh, I really ought to have thought up a more esthetic name for you in the course of the centuries—well, at least I have this name to myself alone, haven't I? Losch has now been rechristened "Bibox," which can be pronounced most meltingly and is expressive anyway. Furthermore he probably won't come to you as he is planning a tour in the Harz. He is not jealous any more—he has understood. Toward the end of the semester we were once on the point of breaking up—he began going to the café day and night and in consequence was quite utterly limp in his non-café life. Well, those are the cares of married life. But I believe the mutual ill-humor that stemmed from it will die down in the course of centuries. But *respect* must not be lost, else everything is lost. We have become very much accustomed to each other—there's a danger in that of course, but it prevents us from an I-don't-care–you-don't-care letting the whole thing go the devil. And that would presumably, at present anyway, be stupid—on my part also. This sounds awfully unloving, this intellectual weighing of For and Against—but love—I do not love Losch. I believe one can only love that which one recognizes as superior.

I have been here alone (i.e., with Sonni) since the 9th. At first I had to work off the consequences of a severe influenza I contracted at the end of February skiing (a headlong fall on ca. 20 m and other such pranks). Then I worked—got lazier and lazier—finally enjoyed idling the time way. At last pulled myself together for a tour to St. Peter and St. Märgen with a young fellow as amiable as he was insignificant. Now I'm about to go up the Kybfelsen with Sonni, and want to show her the Solacker too. We must celebrate the 14th and 15th of July this year. Would be delightful if you were here then!

Do you realize that I first met Losch at the Foundation Day Celebration on the 14th? Incredible. Hornvieh, good Lord, how I look forward to seeing you. And yet I am afraid, always thinking you must then notice how silly-stupid and giddy-tomfoolish I am. Look: you set your "real self" and that "which I would like to see in you" in opposition to each other. On this matter I demand emphatically an explanation of at least 8 pages. In the form of an example in subtraction:

$$\frac{\text{Hornvieh, idolized by me} - \text{Hornvieh's real self}}{?}$$

But now I will go systematically into your long letter. 1) I have with great pleasure discovered a strong vein of irony. Have *you ever really* celebrated carnival? Well, then. Yes, I find it highly sensible, letters in diary form. The business has only one hitch: assume I am in a very pronounced mood one day and write it down. When I go at the letter again, perhaps I read over what I wrote. And the letter strays into the waste-basket. Anyway that's the way it will be mostly, and the more, the more unreservedly I had put down everything in the sense of my mood, i.e., the more valuable the letter was as a letter . . . ?

Evening

So, I went up alone. There is no other place so beautiful, so happy-makingly beautiful, as the Solacker. Brought back a great bunch of pine, holly, and pussy willow, at which all the Philistines I met felt themselves called upon to laugh. Let them—

My dear, I have so much to say and to ask that I hardly know where to begin.

To start with, as I began to idle and consequently to be bored, I went to the theater again. Twice. First Wildenbruch: *Die Lieder des Euripides* ["The Songs of Euripides"]. Not worth anything of course, begins in the style of Iphigenia and ends like an average operetta. I was clear about that from the start. But I hadn't seen a play for 2 years—and earlier on the theater was my all, my home, my

[190]

passion—and the thing took such hold of me that in the
intermission I asked my companion not to talk. *On revient
toujours à ses premiers amours.* Yes, I do still believe today
that I could have done something on the stage—but don't
be scared: I shan't be running away from you all any more.
Am too old and sensible. Yet I was pleased afterward that
I am young enough to let myself be so completely carried
away by the lovely make-believe, so thrilled—God, what a
child! Well, to go on: I naturally went soon again: *Hedda
Gabler.* My illusion gone. Terribly played. Hedda conceived
from only two points of view—as prospective mother and
as cocotte. O Lord! So had leisure to reflect about the play.
As I was going home the question pressed itself upon me:
is that art? It is really only a pathological question drama-
tized! And if that is art, what is Wallenstein—Iphigenia—
Faust?? Is there any absolute scale of values? What does
"artistic value" mean? I am convinced there is one, *must*
be one. But I can't find it. It can't be purely formal—for
with "structure" or "dialogue" alone it still isn't done. This
is a question that has busied me for a long time. With the
books I read too. Just now I have *A Night's Lodging* in
hand. As writing with a social purpose it is of course very
interesting, and it is also from a purely human angle interesting to see what people are like who are destitute of
every convention and every hope—but that surely doesn't
make it art. A dictum of H. Lorn's comes to mind: he had
noticed

> that poetically pleasing is simply
> what everyone has already experienced
> and no one has yet said.

And I must say, if I approach any literary creation it is
with the question: what ideas has the poet or the writer
about people and human life, about this or that struggle
which happens to preoccupy me? Or else I can find in the
work some sort of tone that is sympathetic to me (Storm

sometimes, Turgenev always, or often some little lyric poem). But what I lack is a yardstick that is safer than mere feeling.

I come to you with such naïve confidence in all my troubles—don't laugh at me.

Am tired now but I'm not sending the letter off yet. Good night.

Was away 2 days with the same young man—Wald-kirch—Simonswälder Tal—Furtwangen—Prechtal—Elzach. More than 5 to 6 meters, deep snow. My dear, I had never thought there were such regions here as, for example, the Wildgutach valley. It was pretty strenuous on account of the snow. But glorious. I'm burnt a deep red-brown. At noon we lay in the sun and ate our provisions. Yesterday our resting place was a little pine wood, snow all around, on a slope—in it a little round clearing in full sun, moss-covered, with a few great stones; and my only wish was to lie there for my whole life, staying in the sun.

2 April 1907

My dear,

I came back last evening from a wonderful 3-day tour through the southern valleys of the Black Forest and found your letter.

I hardly dare to speak of what you have confided to me. Surely it is something sacred for you! But I *thank* you! The poems—such deep distress rings through them—why couldn't you make her happy? Do you believe a woman's suffering can be so great that a man's love could not encompass it? You must have loved her differently from the way she loved you—one hears that in your "Song of Farewell" ("Give me once more"—). How remarkable, that love and suffering lie so close to each other. Perhaps it *must* be so, because becoming *one* is probably just an illusion and we want to take it into a reality. My dear, the poems keep ringing in my ears, one especially holds me spellbound with its anxious melancholy and its seductive sound: "Gently from the branch release"—

Tell me more about her—if it is not too hard for you to speak of this woman who brought you such great happiness and so much anxious suffering. I know, of course, that the deepest things are the most difficult to speak of. Even priests leave what is sacred in the sanctuary—

That you sent me the poems! They are a part of you— and so I will protect them devoutly. I won't speak of them any more; perhaps that would only hurt you.

Evening

The two young scamps came whistling (my tour companions) and disturbed us. But the evening belongs to you now. —I have read the Martin. It naturally put me off at first—and even now I can't help an uncomfortable feeling when I read here and there in it. If I should express myself biblically, it would be to the effect that "one does not put new wine into old bottles, and one does not set a new patch on an old garment." But if one takes away this *form* from the book what remains? Certainly the grand-scale ideas remain; but these ideas hardly offer anything new, they live in all of us who strive for intensity in our lives—they have already been expressed more or less, if not often in this peremptory manner. Or am I wrong? What do you say to it? In any case it would interest me very much to hear how this singular book was brought about!

If *we* had been able to go off together now! That we would have enjoyed—the two young scamps were very nice, but—Now maybe nothing will happen about your coming in summer!! You are copying me—promise and then thumb your nose. Otherwise *I* will certainly come in August. But this time no backing out.

And on Good Friday you went off and let everything that
was burdening you be sunned away. Yes, I know, a couple
of those warm rays of the sun can really make one in-
tensely happy. You know, we'll go to Persia and become
sun-worshippers. What was I doing on that morning? Something prosaic and unimportant: I sat me down at the sunny
window and fixed myself up a summer hat—or really that
isn't prosaic—the whole presentiment of summer lies in it,
in the straw, the ribbon, the flowers. See, you now know
why I haven't written for such a long time—no, it wasn't
the "eye-ology," I have done devilishly darned little so far.
Haven't had a qualm of conscience on account of that—
it was so glorious out in the open and it did me so unspeakably much good. Yes, and then after a trip like that,
I have a sincere aversion to anything printed—and then my
summer dresses all have the characteristic of somehow
looking in need of help.

I also got a long letter from Losch yesterday. I had that
feeling of guilt toward him again, because I do not love him
as he loves me. He writes so beseechingly. I know he needs
me very much now. And I never want to treat him badly,
never. Only by being kind to him can I thank him for his
love. And I really am very fond of him. He is struggling
sincerely to become a whole person, to conquer the vacilla-
tion between art and science that has prevented him from
getting anywhere—in any field. I will write him soon. I
know I can make him happy with a few words. —Bah, a
horrid thought comes to me: is it only this sense of power
that stirs me? —But do we know the source of our
feelings??

I have read Windelband's *Preludes* with *great* interest.
Do you know them? Philosophy again and again has an
irresistible fascination for me—but now, for the rest of
vacation I shall have to work at something real, and philosophy must remain the forbidden fruit—but it is very
tempting.

Both I *cannot* do. When I am working hard I cannot do any heavy reading—and the other way round. —So, but now I must definitely stop. And away with the letter. Why? Because I *look forward* to yours.

And that you know, my dear. You have imperceptibly drawn me into your train of thought. I begin instinctively to defend myself against your influence and your power. Do you understand that? I should simply be happy that you are my friend, Hornvieh, little one, dear one.

Karen.

7 April 1907

My litte Hornvieh,

Outside the rain is falling—quietly—incessantly—disconsolately. I have to come to you, in flight from this eternal greyness. I thought a letter would come from you today. You have spoiled me so—now I get impatient if you let a single day go by. This morning it was simply delightful; the young scamps came along with white carnations in their buttonholes and shiny brand new gloves, and we went promenading together. Music and lots and lots of people in their best—I like that from time to time. In Hamburg I often strolled around the main streets for hours, day after day, senselessly and aimlessly, only driven by the need to be in the midst of the swirling colorful turmoil.

10 April, Laufenburg a. Rhein

Yes, on the Rhine, Hornvieh, dear—and it flows close below my window and swashes over the great gray rock masses, the green Rhine. Opposite a couple of antique, decrepit houses with colorful little wobbly shacks built out in front on the rock. They stand so far back that there is just room for a poor little spot of green. And in a magical thunderstorm lightning and two rainbows like high bridges in the sky.

You think you could surely read all that in travel books too, you scoffer! But you know, that makes me so happy. I could stand for hours at my window or on the old Rhine bridge and forget time and myself. You see, that's why I still must quickly tell you about it.

I wanted to take Sonni out to pasture a bit before the crowd comes back. So we were 3 days in the Alb valley. Oh! And the young scamps with black ribbons on their sticks and flowers with mourning bows at the station!

My dear, is there a letter from you waiting at home for me? Woe to you if not! There's revenge enough in the thought that you have to sit in court (brrr!) and in your room while—oh, pooh, I am just too mean. Comes of having everything so good. Now I would like just to drink champagne and dance all night—perhaps with you. Do you like to dance? Yes, shake your head, little Hornvieh, and sigh with me that there isn't carnival every quarter. Well, now I would like to be sitting on a stool at your feet with you reading aloud something beautiful to me—on the order of a novelette by Jacobsen?: *Roses Should Stand Here*—or something of yours, your letters, all of them. And more of the poems—oh, my dear—up here there is a little church, overhanging a little village, which looks over the crooked alleys, over the red roofs, on the Rhine. It is all white and simple inside, only a couple of colorful frescoes on the ceiling and a golden high altar—that's what it would be like if I heard your voice now.

This morning in the Alb valley a funeral procession came by. A black coffin on the hearse wagon. Only one wreath on it. And the men followed, bareheaded—then the women. The bells sounded from the little mountain chapel and the procession halted before every cross along the way and prayed. At that the bells fell silent each time. —I had to think of our tasteless funeral processions in the cities.

11 April, home again and found a letter from little Hornvieh. And now I don't want to do anything but write to you again right away.

No, a "commentary" to your arguments was not necessary. Perhaps because I have got somewhat into that line of thought through Windelband. With that book, as you wrote me in one of your first letters, everyone must find his own spring-board from which he can plunge into the immeasurable waters of philosophy.

Yes of course you are right—my demand for a self-criticism was absurd. One doesn't do that sort of thing on order—and you don't want to deprive me of the joy of discovery.

What you write about egoism is most valuable to me. I may possibly have *known* it once, but it had not become my own mental property. Look, we so easily come to the following sequence of ideas: as a child one hears about this and that praiseworthy emotion, action, etc. 2nd stage: one comes to understand that, e.g., mother-love, martyrdom have their source in egoistic emotions—or to carry the same idea further, that they run their course just as much according to laws of Nature as rain and thunderstorms. And from this one at first draws the conclusion that mother-love is to be morally evaluated no differently than murder in a robbery. I drew that conclusion earlier. One mistakes the fact that observation of a causal connection is no evaluation—or, if one has run aground on "egoism" that it depends on the *content*.

I believe a lot has become clearer to me through your letter.

The line of thought that leads to a formulation of "artistic worth" is really quite similar to the ethical. Remarkable.

I think it is fine of you to concern yourself with the workmen. That must give you *great* satisfaction. Wasn't it difficult at first to hit the right tone? I can hardly imagine it. With *women* of lower social standing I can get on quite easily—but women don't really belong to any class, they all belong in one. Much sharper boundary-lines with men. Perhaps this comes partly from women's general lack of education. Compare shopgirl—"young lady." In principle the former is more sympathetic to me, for 1) she is doing something, 2) she isn't polished up with "general education," 3) she knows life.

Yes, of course, I would like to see your friend here. If for no other reason, because he can tell me about you.

But I am frightfully shy—don't laugh, Hornvieh!—I really am. Only not with the few people with whom I feel at home at once—and even there it is still a long time before I have sounded out enough terrain. I have already spoiled a great deal with this not-being-able-to-get-out-of-myself (oh!). But naturally it isn't as bad in writing as orally.

To come back to the book once more. I know the Bible very well, as my father was a strict Christian (or is), but for that very reason it is unsympathetic to me—as if one had a dear old grandmother and one day when one goes to see her she is dressed in a dress of the newest fashion—hm.

Idchen? Developed? No, only that she has found a home here and while she is here feels happy and quiet. She is now writing half-crazy letters from Hamburg, pained by the fixed idea that she can't come back. Poor little thing. I shall be glad when I have both my children here again. She has "increased in wisdom" only in so far—her first love, you know. And perhaps that is the biggest chapter in a woman's life. Mine is still one of my sunniest memories. I was glad when I saw that she had got over that flirtation anyway. But she has *learned* nothing, nothing at all. Perhaps that will come—I hardly think so. It doesn't suit her.

Losch and I? I think I would rather *tell* you about it. And it must be dark then and you may not look at me. No, there is nothing bad about it. But I have often been thoughtlessly lighthearted, and this story demonstrates that very clearly. There are such awfully different sides to me, equally strong, so that a peaceful straight-forward development was precluded from the start—now at least I cannot surprise myself any more.

12 April

Yesterday the young scamps, the wretched fellows, came storming into my room and dragged me off after the first fond greeting to the living room. I shall have to keep them off a little.

Evening

I must have run up and down my room for ½ an hour, transferring my inner restlessness to the outside. I am so dissatisfied with me—I did so frightfully little in the holidays—finally the eternal distraction came along and the tours—today again I have been unable to do any work all day and didn't do any. So, I must therefore write my discontent out of me. And when I have once verified my uselessness by example, it usually goes better. Because such internal quarrels have the same effect on me as quarrels in the house; both unbearable. But: does this feeling of disgust come simply from the drive to activity not being satisfied—or is it a revolt of my conscience at not having fulfilled the duty to work? ?

Why do we so much more easily recognize a logical and aesthetic conscience than an ethical one?

Hornvieh, if I didn't have you—I already feel almost safe, just writing to you.

Is Karl Martin your only "friend"? And the one you were living with, did he move with you? Or why?

Who are your women friends from whom you get letters on Sunday? Tell me about them, will you?!

I am more and more disturbed about Losch. He has once again felt he has the power to be an artist. Now he is wavering. I wrote him he should go the way he could achieve the most according to his own *conviction*. Have no answer yet. If he goes back to music now! I believe he is by nature an artist. But he will perish if he gets into the atmosphere of those artistic circles.

That is probably why I couldn't even now speak to you about Losch + me, because these things trouble me so much. It is no lack of confidence. For in whom could I confide if not in you? And it makes one happy to be able to confide.

My dear, it is late and I want to go to bed. This letter must go, for tomorrow I want to work. Funny, I have to fight this decision and yet I know that I shall enjoy it. So you'll also be getting my letter in the Sunday mail! Oh! Spoiled little beast! I see you sitting at your desk, caressing the letters with an expert's glance—which one first?

Well. Goodnight!—or rather good morning, little Hornvieh!

Karen

Freiburg, 1 May 1907

My little Hornvieh,

I wrote you a long letter a few days ago—and have just torn it up. There was something in the air that depressed me—I kept getting more tired and apathetic. So I finally sat down and confided everything to you. Losch got wind of it and made me promise not to write you about it. Possibly I wouldn't have sent it off anyway. There just are things about which one must not speak even with those dearest to us. And then—it was a matter between Losch and me. May I talk about *that* with *you*? Isn't that a sort of—deception? I would resist if Losch had a girl-friend to whom he told everything, even about me. That one can hardly conceive of, the way he and I stand to each other, not conceivable because it is *I* who am his girl-friend. We would then soon again have happily arrived at the question of exclusivity, only that it is now easier for me to grasp— unfortunately. Does a collision always have to enter into it, even if one is close to only 2 people? I don't mean an external collision—but in such a way that between each two there exists a secret bond of which the 3rd party knows relatively little. That was borne in upon me because he attacked me in a commanding tone: "are you writing the Hornvieh about me?" And I had to admit he had a certain justification—and tore up the letter.

And now—now I hardly have the impulse to write you. The thought that you will come in July already makes me quietly happy—and if anything troubles me, I postpone it in thought to that time. Two days ago there suddenly appeared a fellow from our circle in Hamburg who was the first to stimulate me. I was glad when I heard of it, for with him there came back a whole world of memories of that blessed period of awakening. Yes indeed, and so he came.

Oh! Long, well-groomed hair, posing in every way as "an important man." First I had him tell me about my little friend Rolf (I have already told you about him), and heard that he had become always more unapproachable and had fallen out with a number of people. That concerned me very much. Why didn't I stand by him in those days? I was very fond of him and knew what I meant to him. I believe that is the only step in my life that I sincerely regret—and accordingly I have a burning wish to be able to make good to him for it. But reproaches and wishes: all vain. Not to be thoughtless at the right moment, that is what it comes down to. I have now finished writing down everything I knew and thought about Rolf and me—it has come to over 70 closely written quarto pages. Gave me pleasure, that work.

But to go on about the aforementioned young man with

the long hair. I went for a walk with him. For an hour. You know, I was perfectly blissful when I saw Losch again and Venus (a medic, mutual friend of Losch and mine, clever, lazy, moody, most genteel), the fellow had chattered so all the way. He "philosophized." Hornvieh! The thought of you was a comfort and release, to prevent my arriving at the idea that all "philosophizing" people are chatterboxes. (Another of the kind recently fell into my hands.) Hornvieh, dear, that you exist makes you worthy of adoration! So it mattered nothing to this young man that he promptly introduced himself as a "convinced Häckelist" without having any idea of what "monism" really meant, flung Kant to the metaphysicians, cooked psychology and philosophy in one pot like cabbage and potatoes. Well, I really admired myself for not attacking him. Moreover, he naturally had the intention of later on favoring the world with a philosophic work!

Once I had got over my rage, of course, I couldn't stop laughing all the rest of the day.

I asked myself with a shudder whether they were all of the same caliber in those days! But am wary of flatly affirming that since it would be too humiliating for me. But *quidquid id est*, those people were once able to give me something, so peace to their ashes!

I have a lot of interesting lectures this summer, looking forward above all to anthropology and ontogeny. Then anatomy *in vivo*, which I had objected to for a long time out of embarrassment—but one has to deposit little-girl feelings outside the door of anatomy. Most of it is probably acquired prudery, which has little to do with modesty and is hardly justified. Evenings 2 times per week I drum physics and chemistry into the two of them, as Losch is just too naïvely ignorant therein. Have also read a book on electricity. Very interesting. —Idchen is working! I hope she will stick to it. For the rest our doll house is re-established, only that now it carries more the stamp of serious work.

Hornvieh, you are coming, aren't you? Do you want to stay in Güntersthal again? I have an instinctive antipathy to the fellow to whom the hotel belongs. But your room was charming. —But what a pedant you are! I'm pouring the whole bowl of my abhorrence into this sentence.

4 May, presumably

Hornvieh, little one—the sun is shining, and I could lie in my armchair for an hour and only feel that it is light and warm and comfortable. The others have gone to Güntersthal. Mother is sick, so I can't very well leave but must more or less play housewife, cook, and the rest of it. Now I want to use the undisturbed quiet to write to you. Last time I stopped, Losch had come in. He wanted to read the letter. He didn't want to share me with you and the like. Of course, I brought him to reason. —My dear, I don't think much will come of this letter today, for I am dead tired— am not used to all the work in the house any more. And then I get that painful feeling, of which I am now more, now less conscious—that I lack something. What, I cannot put into words. Perhaps a sort of blurred, vague idea that all this is still not what is called "living." That sounds like a longing for the rush of an exciting life. But is rather the contrary. Quiet, peace, harmony. Perhaps it comes from the fact that those around me have a fundamentally different way of attacking life.

How else could I explain it fully and at length, whereas I would find it difficult to characterize it briefly, since I just don't know where the essential point of this difference lies. Possibly it approaches the difference one used to label realism and idealism. But slogans alone certainly won't do it.

Hornvieh, I am too tired. Now I have time and quiet to write, which seldom happens these days, so I don't always want to hear: are you already writing to Hornvieh again! And now I am not fit to write. Be nice and write me instead! Will you? And a really long letter, please. Oh well, the perforation *doesn't* clarify anything for me, as it doesn't beautify the letters (in spite of an eventual pink silk ribbon) and I can find my way in them as it is. Amen.

I have the impression that there isn't a single sensible word in this whole letter. The next will have more content. But now I must have another letter from you. Yes indeed. I remember when your last came. I had just waked up, and it lay on my heart like a mountainous burden that my dentist would be torturing me in a few hours. And then Sonni brought me your letter. Whereupon the barometer of my mood shot up and even the dentist appeared to me in a milder light. And when I got to him trembling, he thought we could leave things as they were for the present. I could have embraced him with delight—I'm an infuriating coward where such murderous instruments are concerned! Well, and I naturally thought nothing could be bad today when the day began so well.

If anything I had on had enough buttons, I would count off: shall the letter go into the envelope or into the waste-basket? Various things seem to me wrong in it, or rather one-sided and so raising false notions, e.g., that I am running around here terribly unhappy and with a black dress and ditto face. Well, the notions are your affair. And it doesn't really matter—or does it? But *write me.*

Karen

11 May 1907

Thanks for everything, little Hornvieh!

First, here are the poems back. I'll write when I have some peace. It was dear of you to write so soon and so fully. Amusing that we began our letters at the same time. Telepathy? —Furthermore if you will put a little ribbon through right away (different colors please!) the punching of holes is very easy. See, I'm already getting shameless.

In contrast to which I was dragged along to the photographer's today with violence and some smart trickery. In addition, Wednesday after Whitsun for a 4-day trip in the Vosges. Serves you right! Shame on you! You little dung-bettle, you must come in July, won't you?

Well. That's probably all that can be taken care of in provisional telegraphic style. But don't talk to me about gross ingratitude, sir! This of course doesn't represent an "answer." It is too hot, and Saturdays the ladies' bath is not open. Scandalous! Tomorrow I shall greet Kandel Mountain for you and with the last snow up there, in all respect, knock your hat off your head. So long till then. Think of me occasionally meantime.

Your Karen

Freiburg, 25 May 1907

My little Hornvieh,

Please appreciate that I declined an invitation to a wine-punch in the Kopfgarten with music, in order to write peaceably to you. That is to say, I will not begin the letter with a fib, even if it's only half a one. I am fed up with the others (except Losch and Idchen in part) after we have been on a 4-day trip together. The one to the Vosges, you know. It is a blasphemy to be five on a trip in the Vosges. Two at most, or at least two *at best* assuming that the two are attuned to each other. The way it's best to go to the theater alone. There must be no break in the mood, and one should not have to spend part of one's strength eliminating —mentally—the others. If Venus, for example, threw stones at frogs at the Lac des Corbeaux—all right. Do you

know this little lake? Losch measures Nature only by the
yardstick of the grandiose—a good Alpine view can drive
him wild with enthusiasm. He has no sense of the idyllic.
And I feel admiration for the grandiose, it *elevates* me—
but only that moving, silent beauty, that deep, smiling
peace, as, for example, this little lake exhales it, makes me
happy. Then another thing on which Losch and I never
agree: my lack of group spirit, as he calls it; my keeping to
myself, for instance, as we walked the crest of the Belchen.
I find that so long as it doesn't do the others any real harm,
each one should do what seems to him best. For example, a
reproach aimed at this point will not be omitted because
this evening I didn't want to go along. I do not see the sense
of demanding that in disputed cases I should join the
majority. Perhaps this fits in with my having absolutely no
feeling for blood-relationship. What do you think? Is this
lack of *esprit de corps* a real lack on my part or is it
justified?

I think a weighing of interests should take place here:
do the others lose relatively too much through my acting
in my own way, or does my gain outweigh their loss?

I found your card here. I have heard nothing from Lisa
yet, but *it goes without saying* that your friends are dear
to me and I "help and serve them in all the necessaries of
life." For the rest, a good flower shop is Hofmann,
Kaiserstrasse 71.

Now after the trip my soul is filled with beautiful pictures
that have impressed themselves upon it. That gives me a
feeling of secret joy, as though I carried a talisman with me.
I look forward to an outing with you, Hornvieh—look, it
bothers me when somebody is with me who would really
rather eat a good dinner than be walking in the open. How
is it with Braunschweig, that godforsaken nest where
Nature is concerned. Geography was never my strong suit.

[206]

Isn't it somewhere near the Harz? Don't laugh if that's wrong!

My dear, I believe I did something quite improper last week. It was an act of vengeance against my brother. He sent me the rough draft of a letter I was to write to his girl-friend so that she should feel free to make a trip with him at Whitsun. You know I have no moral objection against it. But I didn't do it. And that because at the time of my intimate friendship with little Rolf he gummed up a meeting with him (he was in Berlin and we were to meet in Wittenberge) out of *pure malice*, i.e., because Rolf, being a Jew, was unsympathetic to him. And it was a noble friendship based on intellectual community of spirit—while his affair is a thoroughly inferior relation aiming at the satisfaction of his vanity and his sensuality.

And: through my negative attitude his plan was only made more difficult, not spoiled. He has always behaved unfairly toward me, while I was stupid enough to more or less fall in with his intentions. And now the whole old grudge awoke that had slowly but surely been storing itself up, and—yes—I took a grim pleasure in his hellish anger at my attitude. It is all very understandable, isn't it? But as your friend would say: it was an act of the flesh and not of the spirit. Or is revenge ethically justified? No, that I would instinctively like to deny, when I think of the diabolical and yet rather uncertain joy I experienced in the event. But the indictment might very well be upset by the circumstance that in one's revenge one gives up one's higher ethical standing relative to the other person, isn't that so? Then it is probably a vain labor of love to attain absolution for ourselves through such and similar sophistries.

You may be thinking after all that it would still be worthy of appreciation that I should have any moral compunctions because of this affair. But the enormously dangerous thing is that my entire entourage is thoroughly amoral, so that

now and again I have to begin like a schoolboy with his
ABC and ask myself whether these people are not right
after all when they disavow outright any higher point of
view from which we should test our inner selves, considering this requirement absurd and unnatural. Add to this
that I too for a time was thoroughly unscrupulous in
ethical matters. And I fear there is some truth in *semper
aliquid haeret* [something always persists]. Even now I
have days of total indifference in *puncto* morality and total
thoughtlessness. I say: even today—and that means you,
Hornvieh, for who knows whether without you I would
have been able to pull myself together, little Hornvieh.

26 May

Something very weird happened to me on the trip. I have
an old teacher on whom I once had a "crush" and who is
still very much attached to me. I haven't thought of him for
a long, long time. His birthday is on the 25th of May and
he would miss a greeting from me on that day very much.
The night of the 23rd I dreamt about that man—and so
did not forget this pious duty. Silly, that, perhaps not worth
telling you. But still—there remains an unresolved remnant
of the uncanny. Our life is indeed built in an insanely
complicated way—and nobody has ever had greater pity
for himself than I, since I ought to have understood it and
couldn't—but such accurate storing-up in memory and
such automatic emergence at the right time is, to say the
least, incomprehensible. You know, Hornvieh, I have
worked terribly hard on the brain, but now the thing begins
to take shape plastically before my eyes. It was pure joy of
discovery as one point after another became clear. The
practice of chemistry is enchanting. You do understand a
little chemistry, don't you? They leave us more or less to
ourselves, but since I already know a little about it, it
amuses me to dig through the whole tangle on my own
hook. I think I would die if I should now stop studying
medicine. At bottom what one does in civil life is probably

[208]

a secondary matter—but that I now have work that I love and an aim gives me something firm outside myself that I can reach out and hold to, even in my abysmally black states of mind. The Gymnasium offered me nothing of the sort. My dear, what are Grete and Lisa in civil life? Or is that irrelevant for them?

I can so well picture Lisa to myself from your description, especially as I know a woman who must be like her in nature. People whom she must resemble have something unspeakably touching for those of us who are more robustly built, they arouse a mixture of respect and shy sympathy, and because we set them high, higher than ourselves, the sympathy turns into an all-embracing love that selflessly desires only good for those others. . . .

No, Hornvieh, I "do not demand you for myself alone." That would seem to me presumptuous. It is happiness enough for me if you take part in my life, I in yours. "A common, rich, inner life"—yes, Hornvieh dear, you are right. What you say always sounds so true and simple, you know, in the manner of "you speak a great word unconcernedly." So. I know it is a great happiness when this common inner life is limited to only two—but as nothing in Nature is handed to us as a gift, so this "happiness" too is linked with renunciation that—perhaps—outweighs it. My dear, what you couldn't write me, you will tell me. You know, I see it coming: we shall have so much to tell each other that we will be wrapped in deep silence. By the way, there now exists a good, as they say, picture of me. Perhaps. But I also want one of you! *Potsdonnerwetter!*

5th page; I have a real writeritis, and it goes so fast that you may need weeks to decipher it.

You know, little Hornvieh, it goes strongly against the human grain in me to write you about Losch + me. And it is difficult to fight off something like that on logical grounds. Yet I am convinced that shred by shred I shall gradually tell you everything. Possibly the fact that I am not so crystal clear about the "Karen-Losch case" that I could speak of it objectively, may play a role in this. But just here is where you could help me—to be clear. You reproach him for his love not being sure enough. Is that *his* fault? No. For presumably it would be sure if *I loved* him fully and wholly.

He doesn't know me? In any case there are sides to me that are incomprehensible to him and hence in part unsympathetic—that is, tritely put, that I think about and grapple with things that one cannot touch and put under the microscope like a beetle or some other insect.

Perhaps that's just the best thing about me, which he so misconstrues—but still it is only a *part* of me. And of this he is at least not intolerant, indeed I believe that he—perhaps unconsciously—acknowledges in this very point my superiority to him, generally speaking. Whereas I can be nothing to *him* in what *he* has most at heart, in music. From which it may be seen that *neither* of us can give the other anything in what is most important to us. That looks rather sad. But in everything that lies below this top story of our souls we fit more or less well together. This is not irony on my part, my dear, even though it sounds somewhat like it. It is just a compromise (inferior word, and still more inferior matter!), preferring to take what is good when one doesn't have the best, instead of declining everything with thanks and doing without. Perhaps you will attack this point of view, but I have a number of defensive weapons ready for that case.

You see that I feel my affair is standing on weak legs, because I immediately think of defense. He does not know himself? That is *not* the case. He has a pretty strongly developed sense of self-criticism and knows himself, his capacities and his limitations, *very* well.

I must help him and be his friend? But that I am doing, can be, and am. It is probably the maternal element, which so often lies in a woman's love, that comes strongly to expression in our relationship.

But my longing for higher things—that has little to do

with him. Note: "little," not "nothing." There is so much about him that is lovable: his childlike quality, his bashfulness before big words, his basic honesty, which disdains his making more of himself than he is, the generous framework of his character, and his *keen* mind.

Then there is much in which we complement each other. The way it goes in our studies, I am smarter at more abstract things, e.g., physics, and he is in general quicker at understanding concrete things like anatomy.

Oh dear, this essay isn't finished yet. Cicero is child's play in comparison. Well: that's the way it goes with a lot of other things in daily life.

Then another thing: his love for me is touching—and for me that is of incalculable worth. And another thing, about which one does not speak easily but which still—especially with a woman—should not be overlooked: he gives my senses such a measure of nourishment that they do not upset my inner equilibrium through pangs of hunger. Is that cynical? I don't really know. You may criticize.

So, Hornvieh. Now you know a lot about the matter and can probably make yourself an approximate picture. This last should express more confidence in your capacity for spiritual gropings than in the virtue of my description.

And now to end. For the rest, physics for Losch at Easter, for me next summer.

Are you coming in July?? Do make your paper a few pages shorter! Oh Karen! This time it's a letter cast in a single mold. I have not read it over. I believe it might otherwise seem to me too embarrassingly honest. I greet you, dear little Hornvieh.

your Karen

27 May 1907

The other letter has hardly gone off, and here I already sit again despite resistance, writing to you.

And perhaps it will just be a diary scrap. I feel as if yesterday and the day before I had taken pleasure in showing you myself from an ugly side. Am I sorry? No, indeed not. For *because* you understand the *good* in me, I have a burning wish that you should know me wholly, wholly. Why is it so unutterably beneficial, the thought that somebody besides myself knows me?? Do I only want your opinion about me, my value? Hardly. But what is it then? Tell me.

When I am just a little bit tired I am absurdly vulnerable to small acts of tactlessness. I was sitting in the living room today, reading a book of Gabriele Reuter, the basic thesis of which was sympathetic to me. Then Mother began to talk about the book and Losch to deliver a ponderous review of its train of thought. I went out, not to get rude. Losch is almost never tactless—but only almost. Worth appreciating, for there are few people of whom one can say that. Tact is conditioned by an intensive empathy with the state of the other person, or it can also be conscious, hence clever people are seldom tactless if they don't want to be.

This evening I shall spend with Eric, friend of my youth. We used to play theater and Indians together. We were like brother and sister. It was never a very deep relationship, but at times quite intimate. My feelings for him have never changed. Once on a warm afternoon in May—he had played me Beethoven and I had recited a couple of lovely poems—we kissed. Just quite naturally. It had to be. I thought no more of it and had almost forgotten that moment—and he had loved me then. I didn't even notice that at the time, so our sibling relationship remained unclouded.

[212]

He told me about it later, when he had overcome this strange emotion. Last summer we had a day together in Berlin and went to the heath. There was always understanding between us without many words. Now he has been in Berlin 3 years and appears to be—no, not corrupted, but heavily besmirched by what goes on there. I sensed that instinctively the moment he got here and could not overcome a coolness in my behavior toward him, so that we have hardly talked with each other. But I have seriously undertaken not to let myself be prejudiced by that impression, and must test out whether the good kernel in him remains. And I almost *believe* so. For a clean person always remains basically clean, even if he has bathed in filth. That is my conviction.

31 May

Little Hornvieh is beginning to frighten me. No, actually I feel uneasy. For one thing, I wrote you on your birthday —look at the date on which I began this letter. That was your birthday itself! And my thoughts really were with you on that day!

All chance? Every other explanation is unsympathetic to me—but . . . brrr.

Now this greeting, contrary to intention, must go off at once and tell you my congratulations in words so that you are aware of them.

The photographer will send the picture.

Greeting
Karen

Freiburg, 6 June 1907

My little Hornvieh,

When I read in your letter that I deserved another entourage, I felt it almost—presumptuous. And now there is
only one question in me that recurs again and again: why
haven't I a single person here, just one, who could be my
friend? There are moments when I hate the others—a mild
feeling of contempt seldom leaves me. And then—this belongs to it—it practically lies in the nature of the case that
the three stand together against me in all and everything.
Not that they don't love me. On the contrary: I am the one
who receives the most love from the others, and a "friend"
actually spoke today of a Karenocentric system. These
external irritations come from a difference of principle in
the concept of living together, about which I have already
written you, but which I can now formulate better. Losch
says that when three want something and the fourth
doesn't, the fourth should in any circumstances acquiesce
(in all social doings, amusement, etc.)! I say it doesn't
matter *how many* want something, but what the individuals
want.

For example, if the others want me to play cards with
them and I am working, work takes precedence. Now Losch
is just as convinced of his own viewpoint as I am of mine.
In consequence of which I am daily obliged to hear that I
am unkind, single-track minded, that I "always" separate
off, and want something special for myself. Well, let them
talk! But this eternal nonsense really does make me unkind
in the long run.

For the rest, if I wrote about hatred and contempt, this
does not apply to Losch. And the other two? Want me to
characterize their immorality? I would rather let you judge
for yourself and will give a few examples as objectively as
possible:

Idchen once came to know a young fellow, rather dreamy

and poetic by nature, who thought he had found an understanding soul in Idchen and paid her homage accordingly.
He wrote her letters into which he apparently put his
deepest thoughts and feelings (even if they did undoubtedly sound rather overwrought). Idchen made the
greatest fun of him—but answered him in his own style,
so that she kept his belief in her awake although she
knew that he fundamentally misunderstood her.

Idchen has a sister who has in her make-up all that is
worthless in Idchen raised to a higher power and nothing
else; she is heartless, a coquette, calculating, and false.
Until Idchen had been made aware of this absolute worth-
lessness by someone else, she thought more of this sister
than she did of herself *because* she had "more success with
the gentlemen" than she herself.

This sounds like a severe indictment, it sounds like the
prayer of the Pharisee in the Temple: I thank thee, Lord,
that I am not as they. The question also occurs to me: how
is it that you see the mote in your brother's eye—?

Am I justified in these complaints? Yes, I am, for I am
just as severe with myself. *Only for that reason.* Well, now
the thoughts about my thoughts have been happily con-
veyed to paper. —So now we go on or this will become a
critique without end as in Marianne Sinclair. (Do you know
her? In *Gösta Berling*? If not, read it please please! For a
rest! In Switzerland! It's one of the most wonderful
books I know.) So, to go on. (In a German composition
"Thema!" would be written in red ink in the margin.) Sincerest thanks to heaven, I don't need to write any more
German compositions for German high school teachers!
Instead (nice transition, isn't it?), instead I am writing to
little Hornvieh and will now dig out a few educational
examples of Sonni's from the treasury of my memories.

A detail comes to mind from the time when I was a child
and incomparably more consistent in things ethical than
now.

I had heard in church and at home from Mother about "Christianity in action," and it became immensely clear to me: be not only bearers of the word, but doers. Whereupon one Sunday I stuck my savings of 50 pfennigs in the church box—and at home was scolded for it by Mother.

Of course she wants a wealthy marriage for Berndt. When he was having to do with a lot of shopgirls, she was not bothered by it. That he now has *one*, whom in his own way he loves, she finds that very disturbing. And even if neither the one nor the other state makes any demand on ethical value, the second without any doubt is the higher. Fear of the depths! In a way one can also bring up here the fact that she silently overlooks my brother's meannesses, while at an unfriendly word from me she loses her temper. Incidentally: I am *really not* of a lovable nature, I mean even where it is not just a matter of fighting for a principle. A lack I am trying to get over but am not yet finished with. She often used to spur us on in lying to the old gentleman, while at another time she would insist to us that lying was something bad.

At bottom she is a good person, only in ethical things, though gifted with good insights and good will, so incredibly inconsistent and thoughtless.

Hornvieh, my brother—he was formerly my idol. Recently he has given me a chance to look into the depths of his soul. And I saw abysmal meanness and an ignoble disposition. It was so low that I was quite stunned and kept thinking only: it is impossible for anyone to be so mean. And my brother at that! It is too long to tell you the story. I felt bruised all over. Losch says this probably comes of my "always going around with such ideal people, like Hornvieh."

—Oh well. No, little Hornvieh, my moral alarm clock, my dear, I should inveigh against your sermons!

Just go on telling me, say it in every letter in other words. I will never scold about it, not even make fun of it, but make a curtsey and say: thank you, my dear, for not

[216]

collapsing altogether, Hornvieh! I am worried about you. For heaven's sake go away on a *trip without books* (legal and heavily philosophical ones!). One recovers with such difficulty and so slowly from such a strike of the nerves! Please, please take care of yourself. Don't you go to bed too late as well? That wears one out so awfully. One should always go to bed by 11 o'clock and to sleep by 11:05. That's what I do. Go and do likewise. I have a strong suspicion that you work deep into the night! Be good to yourself, do you hear?!

My summer plans are: end of July (close of semester!) to Kassel for 2 days, 1) on account of the galleries, 2) on account of dear relatives, 3) because then I wouldn't arrive dead at Braunschweig. Then via Braunschweig to Hamburg. Only a brief stay there of ca. 2 days, and on to Stockholm, where I go to my stepsister Agnes, who is a dear, good girl. And if later at the autopsy her brain should weigh heavy, that would be evidence against the theory that intellect is prop[ortional] to weight. I'll stay there ca. 4 to 5 weeks. Then Hamburg and end of October back to Freiburg. My Hamburg stay would be longer if I got permission to do some dissecting. *Dixi.*

I hope your friend is traveling without his mother. Childish wish of a pious soul. Write me more about his book! But in German, not gibberish! Please do it! At length. Interests me very much (trite expression for: I'm all steamed up about it!). Of course I don't even understand the title.

I believe I shall have to talk some more about Losch. I mean: "he knows himself" means that thanks to his self-criticism he knows about his own capacities, his line of thought, the tone of his feeling, etc. I don't understand how you can bring the "lack of a central will" under this chapter heading??

The concept of a central will, too, I have an inkling of rather than really understanding it. I only want to say (though I don't know whether you understand it this way) that Losch as a whole person is much more coherent than

I, for example. His whole thinking goes in only one direction, which one might call that of natural science (in its deeper sense). Philosophy (especially theories of morality) and similar jocularities he basically (almost instinctively) rejects, because they don't suit him.

18 June

So, here I am again. I have read through what I wrote and find it rigorous. My laxity and indifference are a mockery. You still have your friend with you, don't you? And you are happy to be together again. My dear, in about 6 weeks we'll be seeing each other. Sounds most unlikely to me. I still can't make the idea come alive. Odd.

This morning I had to fight out a fight about Losch. The others had been taunting him with "petticoat government," etc., and wanted to mislead him again into a restaurant life. Ugh Hornvieh, I really did strike a good blow. I didn't want my laboriously built up work to be destroyed by the immature silliness of the others. Losch took it most sensibly, saying the others could think what they wanted to about our relationship. Losch is endlessly dear and kind to me. We have trained each other to be considerate and to chime in with each other, as is proper in every "marriage."

"The danger of suffocating"—yes, I know—it was once there, in the beginning of the winter semester. And then remembrance of the past came quite spontaneously and on the same day your long letter—and with that the *danger* was over. And now, now I only feel sorry about the power I have to use to protect myself.

This power could be used for going ahead. But I *am* going ahead. Ideas, which used to form an indistinct mass in me because they had stormed in on me too directly and too numerously, are beginning to settle and clarify. From time to time, when I become conscious of some bit of knowledge having really become my possession, a rapturous feeling comes over me. I wish I had more time to read and

[218]

to digest what I have read. But my studies actually make more and more demands on me, because the deeper I get into them the more I love them. My dear, what do your studies mean to you?—or should one add: and your profession? Why did you study national economy? And where do you come from anyway? And how old have you got to be? Oh, curriculum vitae nonsense! I . . . was born on . . . in. . . .

Incidentally my brother is taking his assessor's exam next year. I have a horrid fear of any and every exam, even when I'm perfectly sure of myself. For physics we have 2 bets on, one between Losch and me, and one between me and Venus. I win if I have done better, or even as well. Well, one never knows. I expected something brilliant, never-happened-before from my Gymnasium finals. And see, when it was done, it was mere rubbish, so that my director came to me afterward and expressed the fond wish to give me a good thrashing. Tsha!

My dear, I have a "friend" who from the ground up, in *every* littlest corner of her soul, is pure and good, and at the same time clever and tolerant. By nature. She is a wonder to me. I revere her. Her existence is a precious thought to me. She is marrying at the end of July and it is possible I may go to Hamburg for her wedding, which is as unpleasant to me as everything connected with people, dinners, and speeches that say nothing.

That you like my picture naturally pleases me. But every picture has its dangers, because it compels one to fix and nail fast the conception one gets of the person too one-sidedly. Are those here content with the expression? Yes, very. Look, they would hardly love me if they had not to some extent grasped my nature, as I am in other respects neither amusing, nor compliant, nor pretty, nor "afflicted" with any other characteristics worth aspiring to. *Affici aliqua re.*

Na, so long, Hornvieh. Now comes the turn of the

pancreatic gland. Now say something about "the usual 6 weeks" again! You have probably counted up and considered the averages, you incorrigible pedant.

Your Karen

Freiburg, 18 June 1907

Motto: in deep distress I cry. . . .
Tell me:

1) I can be free Tuesday about 5 P.M., Wednesday *perhaps* by 11 A.M.

2) How long does he think he will stay?

3) Where shall I put him up, as I mustn't take him home with me? Güntersthal?

4) I naturally look forward to seeing him, but once again: I am ridiculously shy, which has to be taken into consideration!! Please, lit.[tle] d[ear] Hornvieh, don't laugh, or at least reply!

Your Karen

Freiburg, 19 June 1907

Have just telephoned. There are many applications but still no room free. He must apply soon and give exact day of arrival and length of stay. She couldn't promise just out of the blue. Ergo! Of course we won't bother with any politeness nonsense. Incidentally, Thursday is my lightest day, so would suit me well. Friday isn't so good! I'm looking forward,

Karen

Friday evening [presumably June 21]

The Free Students' great torchlight procession and Bismarck drinking bouts. Drinking bouts up on the *Kanonenplatz*!

Hornvieh, dear little Hornvieh, I am so frightfully happy. I wasn't going to write anything more.

Still. Your friend—Fullbeard—looks so respectable. O Lord! If he were only gone again! Pooh, no, don't be angry, my dear! What a child she still is, isn't she? Oh. Karen pumping up air, I mean courage, to go to the station and speak to a man with a full blond beard: "Herr Müller?" Yes. Embarrassment. Sniffing inside. "Hearty greetings from Hornvieh," etc. "Oh, thanks". Pause. "How is he?" "Pretty lousy." "Oh, I'm so sorry." Pause.

Hee hee, I could roll back and forth on the sofa 3 times with delight when I think of it.

Oh, had I died as a little child! Your letter was delightful with the motto. Of course I'd much rather go out with him. What should I do with him here? Introduce him? Banal phrase? Of course they said: "how remarkable"—and the tone! But let them be! *Potzdonnerwetter*, surely I am my own boss!

"But only one day in Braunschweig!" I'll see about that: "it depends on how nice you are, but at most 2 days"! Yes, great men get quoted!

My dear, I shall denounce you if you write another letter during a trial! Such dereliction of duty, such frivolity, I don't understand you, you will have to become somewhat more pedantic, somewhat more particular ———

Hornvieh, I have to tell you of my happiness. I must have someone who understands my joy. And only you can do that.

Yesterday morning a letter lay at my place at breakfast in a handwriting that seemed familiar. Like yours, but untidier and not so clean. I recognized it: it was from Rolf. I couldn't believe it at first. And then I read it. You know, I have told you what he was to me, how I have loved him unalterably always, how we parted on account of a love affair of mine. My feeling for him always remained the same, and I could not see how he could wipe me out of his life. For that he tried to do. Since the break I have often tried to bring us together again, but he brusquely turned me down every time. In the end I finally had to resign myself and decide to go on loving him for my part and to honor his memory like that of a loved person who has died. Only this ending to our friendship dimmed the memory-picture and cast a shadow on his character.

And now at last—it is two years since the break—he writes, as I had at the time often hoped, and asks whether we shall try to be friends again, enter into the inheritance of our former friendship.

Hornvieh, I haven't been so over-happy for a long time, so full of inner jubilation. I haven't worked all day and only given myself over to the joy. Joy that I have him again, that I can expiate my guilt toward him, and above all that my belief in the perpetuity of our friendship has triumphed.

I would rather not have spoken to anybody here about it, because my happiness was too sacred. But I felt in duty bound to tell Losch. I had to seek *permission* to write back to Rolf. It was hard for Losch. I had probably hoped too much that he would *understand* my *boundless* joy. But he only thought of the possibility that Rolf might assert older rights and that would be more than he could take. I first had to assure him that this was not the case and yet be grateful that he allowed me to answer. Very likely too much was being expected of him. Yes, that was probably it.

Sonni, who had seen from whom the letter came, expected me to "confide in her," which I was careful not to do as I know how totally she misunderstands Rolf. Now she is offended and sulky. Is she trying to win my confidence that way? Yesterday afternoon I was advised: "for goodness sake don't begin again with that fellow!" Well. I was happy—and for that one always has to take something into the bargain.

I must go to a lecture, Hornvieh, dear, rejoice with me!

Your Karen

27 June 1907

My little Hornvieh,

I was heartless enough at first to double-up with laughter over your description of being sick. Till finally my better feelings came through and manifested themselves in heartfelt sympathy. I will give this letter to your friend. He is not here yet. Will probably come tomorrow or the day after.

But I am glad that in this way you are forced to relax intellectually.

Little, dear Hornvieh! I am so happy. All the vexations of daily life seem to me inessential. And when something threatens to depress me I think: Rolf wants to be your friend again and then I must at once put on a sunny expression.

I also believe that Rolf's and my friendship has now been ennobled; for I think that he will now have understood that the sensual incident was a foreign body in our relation, because sensually we do not suit each other.

Hornvieh, forgive, I speak only of Rolf these days. But surely it is always so that something unexpected, overwhelmingly new, at first preoccupies our whole self.

29 June 1907

So. Your friend is here, he arrived yesterday, Friday evening at 6. I went out to Güntersthal with him. He got the room where you are supposed to have stayed before.

The first evening was, as anticipated, somewhat strained, troubled, at least on my side. It went better today. He told me a lot about his philosophical ideas, and I was naturally grateful for that. For me it is, of course, a rare pleasure to hear a sensible person talk. And I think very highly of him—one can hardly do otherwise, can one? It becomes the more difficult for me to find my way back into my own circle. The tension between Mother and me is getting unbearable. Though nothing, nothing at all special has come up, she treats me like air. Such disharmony in the house is naturally depressing. And the injustice makes me so *angry* that I wish she were dead or far away. Rather live alone than have this dog's life! And one cannot talk sensibly with her—it only makes matters worse. And the reason? "Alienation," we are told. But she lost my confidence and friendship 3 years ago—so why suddenly now? I would be content enough if I found a sensible reason. It is so contemptible and unworthy that every word I say gets turned around, everything I do falsely interpreted on purpose—it's a long time since I've been so truly furious.

I am so downed by all these exasperations that I have to think steadily about you and Rolf, not to drown in my own anger and not to lose all joy in life.

Tomorrow your friend and I get together again. But I am so depressed I can hardly look forward to it.

I will take it as payment for the joy in the renewed friendship with Rolf. I would gladly sacrifice still more for that. In this way it becomes bearable.

This letter must get off today. I have been reproaching myself for not writing you at once, since I know that you are sick in bed and are waiting for a greeting from the two of us here.

Don't tell me you took *any books* with you to the hospital. He also said: "It does too much." Yes. "It." Isn't that delightful? He always speaks of you as "It" in analogy with "das" Hornvieh. Oh. Promptly adopted by me.

So farewell, you dear little neuter! And write soon how you are getting on! We are anxious indeed about "It." The dear!

Your Karen

Freiburg, 30 June 1907

[POSTCARD]

Dear little Hornvieh,

Well, well, what are you up to?! Of course I expect microscopic preparations! My dear, it is awfully nice here, and I am making shy beginnings not to be so shy any more. Furthermore there is a letter for you lying, no, not at the post office, but in my desk. Get better.

Karen

Dear Hornvieh! We are philosophizing in fine style. I'll soon be done in. Karen is great, it was very difficult for her to get used to me at first. I hope your illness is not of a serious nature. I wish you a good recovery. . . .

Sincerely your Karl

Freiburg i Br., 1 July 1907

Little dear Hornvieh,

I suppose I should favor you for a little as long as you are ill, shouldn't I? So I'll sit down and prattle to you about something or other.

First about the days with your friend. I *am* grateful, after the event, that you sent him to me. It is so enormously valuable for me to be together with such a far-thinking person, because there is nobody in my entourage who could set me an example. I have something like admiration for Karl U. We talked about every conceivable thing, i.e., for the most part he to me. The days were very valuable to me in any case. As to his health, he seemed quite well except for his unhealthy color. He thought the excitement of the trip had artificially raised the level of his nervous activity.

I never quite lost the feeling that he was a stranger—it is really not unwillingness on my part, Hornvieh, little one —I *can't* do otherwise. I felt again that I am reserved by nature and that I have to force myself to come out of myself in the presence of a stranger. And yet it should not have been hard for me with this clever and understanding person. On the whole I think we could be a great deal to each other on closer acquaintance.

He naturally told me a lot about you and your friends, and especially about Grete and Lisa. Tell me more about Grete some time, will you? I had a different impression of her from Karl U.'s report than from your on the whole very general picture of her. Would you perhaps like to send me one of her letters??

My dear, I have discovered a new definition for "love." It doesn't contribute anything new, of course, only seeing the old things from another point of view. Shall I run through it for you? (It's really more for a chat than any serious testing!) Then look: I automatically give my self differently to different people. It is incidentally amusing to put the different opinions together.

The old aunts in Hamburg: "A nice, clever, modest young girl." ("Clever," incidentally, stems from the fact that I am studying!)

Prof. Wendt: Extremely able, brilliantly gifted; but irregular, unreliable, given to extreme moods, and boundlessly arrogant, honest.

Sonni: On the whole good at the core, but extravagant ideas and rather cold-hearted, lack of self-control, not likeable, exaggerated feeling of independence.

Idchen: All feelings, etc., etc.

Various: Careless, tendency to "bum around," gay.

Now I "love" the people to whom I can give myself out of inner necessity (without reflection!), give myself in every part (or could give) as I am. In other words: love is the full potentiality of giving. This is, in the first place, purely derived empirically from my own most personal experience. But I believe that all manifestations of love can be subsumed under it. For *me* this definition has a certain practical value, because it helps me to limit some emotional relationships conceptually.

For the rest, I am beginning to work again and to find a *modus vivendi* with my mother. Above all I am looking forward dreadfully to being with you. But you must be well by that time, little individuum. So hurry up with it! Otherwise I might find myself forced in my kind-heartedness to write you more often, which naturally I would be glad to avoid.

By the way, I prefer single sheets unperforated. When you are here it will be a pleasant and useful occupation for you to bind your letters to me!! Won't it? Get well, my dear.

Karen

3 July 1907

Hornvieh, you dear, forgive my having been able to give you some pleasure and not doing it! Now I have a bad conscience and am sitting down again at once and writing to you. Perhaps it is the logical-practical consequence of a talk with Karl in which we both came to the conclusion that it would be natural and sensible not to write each other so often!

4 weeks more! Period.

You must not be bitter about Losch. I no longer am. Everyone who does not stand on a certain ethical level would have reacted like that to my communication. And since I love what is natural and original in him, I may not judge harshly where he destroys something for me.

After the first rush of happiness, I again feel estranged from Rolf. I can't accept it. Often I have to remind myself of our renewed friendship and that he does belong to the people I feel close to. You see, 2 years of almost absolute separation lie between. How boring that at first you are compelled to tell each other the bare meaningless *facts*, almost like strangers. It puts me in an almost melancholy mood when I think how intimately we had grown together before. And then—if only we could see and speak to each other now! Only miserable letters. I have never before felt them to be such an inadequate substitute.

I believe a general emotional fatigue has taken over in me. I have no strong feelings, and even my senses seem to be dead—when I kiss Losch I do it to please *him*. *I* feel nothing doing it. The only thing I think of with a sort of tired longing is the days with you. I find it almost—no, I will not be weak.

On the 13th of July there is to be a summer fête given by the Free Students in the Kyburg.

Then I'll go dancing.

Have I already written you that I will come via Hildes-

heim? We leave here in the morning . . . I stay the night
in Hildesheim and go on the next afternoon to you.

No, I *can't* write any more, the letter can go. It's so
senseless, since we shall see each other soon.

5 July

It didn't go after all. So here are a few words more.

I am being needled every day to spend only one day in
Braunschweig. She is afraid I will meet Rolf. Quite right.
If I can, I shall do it. Don't know yet. Behind her back
in any case. I'm probably a coward. But when one *knows*
that the battle is useless and only embitters both sides. I
would rather lie 4 times than talk of what is sacred to me.
Do you know Storm's—

Never dissimulate with the truth!
Pain it may bring, but not remorse.
And yet, because truth is a pearl,
Neither cast it before swine.

Wherein the "swine" are not to be taken as so very bad.
But the sentiment fits.

I look very untidy inside. But I don't dare begin to clean
up. Big house-cleaning in the holidays.

How is Karl? Was the trip too much for him? Is the air
up there doing him good? And how are you? Poor boy!

But write me, do. I need it. I'll write when I'll be
coming as soon as I know how I shall travel. . . .

My old man lives in Reinbeck, you see. It depends: 1)
whether I must make an important visit in Hamburg, 2)
whether the old man wants me to visit him, and 3) whether
and where I meet Rolf. Clear as the outline for a composition, isn't it?

Tell the sun it should shine again some day. The weather
has been so leaden for weeks. —Write, little Hornvieh!

Karen

? July

Yes, I'll presumably come August 2nd, Friday, noon or afternoon.

Can't we, *if* the weather is nice (??) go to the heath those 2 days? That's just an idea—forget what the distances are. Am just longing for the heath in sunshine—afraid of hotel waiters. Am tired.

Karen

July 12th, from which it is to be gathered that I wrote the above on the 11th. I still can't say anything definite. Waiting for news about the little saint's wedding. If she marries on the 3rd, my trip will be advanced. *Potzdonnerwetter*, may she have 3 dozen children if she doesn't write soon. At least I know the other point: I shall meet Rolf. Only Losch and you know. That will be almost too much of a good thing: first you, then Rolf. For now I can only look forward to being with you. Seeing Rolf again is full of so much uneasy tension, so much anxiety. He feels the same: he doesn't want to write. We must talk together. —I believe I need rest. And I know I shall feel safe with you.

My dear, we have now known each other one year. I.e., your first letter to me is dated September 5th. Dear, dear, little Hornvieh!

I've just thought it would be nice if you had a letter from me Sunday morning. You will be reremembering me. Those were such enchanting days. Such high-spirited happiness without much reflection, such a lighthearted taking hold of life. In those days I would never have suspected that out of them the whole wealth of the next year would develop. I thought only of fleeting enjoyment—and it became the source of my inmost happiness. My dear, I am so overflowingly grateful to you, little Hornvieh. Now in these days I may be allowed to tell you this. They are special days.

And I am grateful to him too—for his love.

[230]

Toward *both* of you I feel I am the one who takes, who has been given gifts. My thoughts keep wandering—I think back to what you two have meant to me—and only now and again does a single thought come to paper. But you can read.

Venus and Tott just came in with a bottle of champagne. But as Losch has a rehearsal in the Kyburg we will postpone the carousal. Sunday evening Losch and I want to celebrate alone. Monday at the silver wedding there will be a big wine-punch on the Loretto. A pity the 3rd principal character cannot be there—oh, well.

One can still think. I *must* soon know exactly where I stand with the wedding. Then I will write you *at once*. It is only a matter of a small shift, like arriving on the 31st of July instead of the 2nd of August. Well, *so long*! Will just quickly go post this!

You will be here in my thoughts these days. But now I *must* stop. Now just to let you know when! the heath?! If I wrote any more I would only vary the one theme, that I look forward to seeing you.

Karen

Monday, 27 July 1907

My little Hornvieh,

I leave definitely Wednesday the 31st from here and stay until *Thursday afternoon* in Hildesheim. I will come to you by a train you can look up, that would leave Hildesheim around 4 or 5. How long I can stay I don't know yet. In any case I am spending Sunday on the Lüneberg Heath with Rolf. Whether we meet there Saturday evening or not till Sunday morning I cannot say yet. It depends on Rolf. But after all that is irrelevant.

My dear, I am delighted that I can stay with you. I have such a horror of hotels when I am alone in them. I shall surely recognize you?! Yes, I think when I see you I will know that it is you—and then the memory-pictures that had gone to sleep will awaken again. Yes, you are quite right: what we shall talk about together is only a secondary consideration—the fact in itself is precious enough. I also don't believe that our being together will in principle alter anything in the conception we each have of the other. But it will become more plastic, more alive. My dear, how glad I am. O Lord! Frightfully!

I must still tell you something at once as I know it will please you. Losch and I have come much closer to each other. Quite unnoticeably he has developed fabulously much. He has now got so far, for example, that he sees that my friendship with you—with Rolf—deprives him of nothing, instead *enriches him* too. Think of it! It was the evening of the 14th and we were alone on the Schlossberg. Since then our relation has deepened quite *considerably*. Happiness is spoiling me, Hornvieh! It is almost uncanny.

Only so much for today. For I shall be with you soon. With you. Yes. I greet you

Your Karen

Hamburg, 22 September 1907

D.H.,

. . . Glorious weather here today. That makes me long to do some mountain climbing again after all, and for Switzerland. . . . I am looking forward to Sonni and you, to home, to Freiburg, to the mountains. For tomorrow I still have 2 appointments and 3 visits to make! Don't be angry! I have a guilty conscience and shall be glad once I am peacefully seated in the train! Give Sonni a kiss from me! Out here in Reinbeck it is peaceful and quiet. *Auf Wiedersehn!*

Your Karen

Fifth Diary

1910–1911

KAREN WITH HER FIRST CHILD, BRIGITTE

LITTLE IS KNOWN about the years 1907 to 1910. Karen Horney continued her medical studies. In the fall of 1908 she completed her preclinical semesters in Freiburg. Her first clinical semester was spent in Göttingen. She then moved to Berlin to complete her studies there. She married Oskar Horney (the little Hornvieh), a lawyer and economist, in October 1910.

Her father died in Hamburg in May 1910.

Her mother died in Berlin in February 1911.

Her first daughter was born in March 1911.

The fifth diary is not the old diary, her friend to whom she confides and with whom she talks. This diary is notes of reflection to assist in the psychoanalytic therapy that she has begun with Dr. Karl Abraham, Freud's pioneer in Berlin. The questions she asks are questions that belong in the conceptual framework of the early phases of psychoanalytic theories. She is not interested in recording periods of vital intensity and exploration; she is concerned with periods where vitality is at a low ebb, with symptoms that speak of resistance and thus of conflicts emanating from the unconscious. Psychoanalysis in 1910 had barely been imported to Berlin. Dr. Abraham founded the Berlin Psychoanalytic Society in 1908, but in fact he was the only practising psychoanalyst in Berlin until 1912.

Berlin, 18 April 1910

Dr. Abraham says we must now have patience. Till now ideas have come with such playful ease. Now we must wait because the resistances are too great. What more can happen now? I cannot imagine what else he wants to find. He has given me many possible explanations for the states of exhaustion, the inclination to passivity that increases to a longing for sleep—even for death—the same inclination to passivity that governs my love life. The desire for physical and spiritual martyrdom, whence the great attraction brutal and rather forceful men exert on me, the wanting to blend in with the will of a man who has set his foot on my neck, all the same story. The shyness too in part belongs here.

Dr. A. thinks this comes from my first childhood impressions, from the time when I loved my father with all the strength of my passion. I got my erotic ideal from that time. I think of the overly strong attraction Ernst exercised on me, again and again, that clumsy, brutally egotistic, coarsely sensual fellow. I have always wanted to kill my passion for him through analysis. Now I understand that all his inferior characteristics, which I kept before my eyes, did not in the least quench my passion; no, on the contrary: the instincts in me wanted such a man—and my conscious *I*, seeking a man of fine intelligence and discerning kindness, resisted against this in vain. In Oskar I found everything I consciously wished for—and behold: my instinctual life rebels. It feels itself drawn to a Karl U. because it scents the beast of prey in him, which it needs. To Rolf too. When we were together in those days he took an unremitting pleasure in tormenting me. Walter S. once said to him: "You are a sadist." He disputed the point at the time—but I knew Walter was right. On his birthday, when he wanted to take Tobby* away from me and we consequently got into a fight in which he forced me to my knees and after that to lie on the floor, imperiously demanding a kiss as the reward of victory, a crimson glow almost engulfed me and in that instant I loved him. He totally lost his self-control at that moment. Oskar is always self-controlled. Even when he forces me to submit to him— it is never savagery or animal brutality—he is at all times controlled, he is never elemental. For living together, certainly ideal—but something remains in me that hungers.

But I wanted to speak of the reasons for this exhaustion. Dr. A. says that with onanists, after the excitement into which they work themselves, a state of exhaustion usually remains.

Now masturbation plays no great role with me—I may do it at times unintentionally—but as a child I probably did it freely. Later on, in place of physical self-stimulation came the mental: the telling of stories. In its effects this is comparable to the physical stimulation. Here too exhaustion follows after the excitement. There are neurotics in whom this connection is quite simply demonstrated: they have daydreams, their thoughts gradually fly too high, their associations grow wilder, suddenly comes a moment of total emptiness, and after that a great exhaustion. The daydreams have taken the place of childish masturbation, the emptiness—orgasm—here as there, exhaustion. Of course, I don't tell myself stories any more. But the unconscious desires this sort of satisfaction: it produces fatigue because it wants that of which the fatigue is a result.

---

* Tobby was a teddy bear on which she learned to wrap diapers and dress and undress babies. [Ed.]

Berlin, 19 April 1910

If only it weren't for this dreadful fatigue. It lies on my eyelids like lead, they want to drop and stay closed. These days of menstruation are particularly dangerous. The wave of stimulation runs high and, of course, normal satisfaction cannot take place. Perhaps my subconscious has an imperative hankering for some kind of satisfaction? But even if I remind myself of this, it doesn't help. Or do I want to avoid something disagreeable through sleep? But what could that be? Housekeeping? When Oskar said it might be good if I went away for the semester my face lit up. Freiburg! Göttingen! And in the following days I pictured to myself what lodgings I would take in Göttingen, where I would eat, and what sort of faces the professors would make. I wouldn't go to Freiburg . . . too many acquaintances, one can't be undisturbed there. And yet Freiburg—a nameless longing steals, steals into my heart when I think of it. I believe I would kiss the earth of the Schlossberg if I set foot upon it, I would go into the cathedral and kneel down and rejoice in my heart and pray thankfully to— well, to some being my naïve heart needed at that moment, just to be able to say thanks. I would even take pleasure in the black clerics again. I would go to Wiedersheim's course and hear how he says: "Commilitonen!" ["Fellow students!"] And all the fountains, the many-colored tower gates, the narrow winding streets—ah, Freiburg!

But still I would go to Göttingen, perhaps because I crave an indifferent milieu, because I want only something friendly, quiet, peaceful—and not to see some memory laughing out of every corner, and not to think on every path I take: I used to walk here with this one or that one, here we kissed, here we picked raspberries, here we drank a wine-punch. I get so absorbed in it: then do I really want to go away? Does my imagination suggest: there in Göttingen you could be well, as in that first clinical semester? Is it really on this account that I am getting worse?

Berlin, 19 April 1910

When I asked Dr. A. today what more he really wanted to find out in me he said: that is the typical question when resistances appear in the course of the treatment. I was uneasy and embarrassed over the interpretation of dreams. He thinks the resistance may grow stronger before it is broken. That is always so. I am curious.

I often wonder whether I have some need for my illness. To let myself be pampered? In order not to have to work? To avenge myself on Oskar with it? As a child I looked forward to lying in bed at night because then I could be least disturbed in telling myself stories. Is my subconscious now continually trying to bring about this or some corresponding situation so that my dreams can pursue their course undisturbed?

When I pass Karl U.'s apartment I think each time: I really could go upstairs so that he would accompany me to the station or home, but I never do it. When I saw him again for the first time night before last, I was unspeakably happy. I was in bed. When he gave me his hand in greeting I had a strong desire to throw my arms around his neck and give him a kiss. Afterward I just went on being glad that with my freshly washed hair I looked quite well; I didn't say much.

Oskar watched me. When Karl spoke of the chic of Viennese women I thought: if he finds even the chic Berlin women coarse, what a repulsive effect I must have on him. And I was jealous of Idchen. I listened to see how often he would ask about her. His blond hair is so silky-soft. I would like to have stroked it.

25 April 1910

Yesterday morning Oskar told me I had "thrown myself away" because I had so conspicuously flirted with Karl. I felt deeply hurt and went into spasms of sobbing as the deep depression of the morning began to ease. It was an outburst of such vehemence, such despair to the point of mortal weariness, that I could not believe it was explained simply by hurt feelings, particularly as Oskar himself declared that he had spoken in a fit of jealousy and was very sweet to me. In the afternoon great exhaustion followed. Dr. A. found that I had taken it so hard because the rebuke had hit upon a repressed wish, namely the very wish to throw myself away, prostitute myself—give myself to any man at random. Consider the charm the demimonde, etc., has for me. Consider the polygamous leanings and stimuli in my dreams, the pleasure it gives me to be spoken to on the street, etc. In the prostitution wish there is always a masochistic wish hidden: to relinquish one's own personality, to be subject to another, to let oneself be used by the other. Hence again and again the drive away from marriage to the simple surrender, no matter to whom. He said I had revealed this complex to him on the first day through a symptomatic action: I had left my handbag in his office. A lady in whom these wishes were at times so strong that she had to go out on the street and talk to someone or other, had left her purse behind 3 times. He pointed out the interest all middle-class women take in prostitution.

28 April 1910

Recently, as I came from Dr. A., a few verses occurred to me:

You have striven for the human good
in ardent honest measure
but in you rules another will
that scorns the world and labor.

You hoped to give your body only
when your soul agreed to it
but instead yield you did
to nature's deeply rooted drives.

You sought to win the noble prize
to be the master of your whims
and yet your efforts meant no more
than the pleasure of a childhood's dream.

We had been discussing in the session how even in relation to mental activity—working, achieving something—the conscious and the unconscious are at war. The unconscious has only one interest: to appease the impulses that were once active in the child. These impulses are incapable of being educated, have to be repressed and find themselves an outlet in the symptoms of neurosis, a compensation of sorts.

Dr. A. said it would be better if I were away from the whole circle here, isolated. He is probably right. I will try to isolate myself here. Perhaps that will help some. Above all the transference to him would be more complete. If I think of myself as living alone—all my wildest wishes would twine around him.

Now I have poured out to you
my inner pain and soul's torment

that gnawed away my vital strength,
I know it safely kept by you.

All the wild wishes that ever stirred
my daring dreams, my secret aims,
you know them all, my soul is yours,
oh lift its sin and make it light.

And here I am struggling against acknowledgment of the transference? However, not only the positive feelings toward him are there, but also the resistance, a certain aversion. And, of course, he has, so to speak, taken Oskar's place. But the most contradictory feelings concentrate on him.

15 July 1910

I have been so desperate this last week, for the sultry weariness would not give way at all. And for a week I had known once again what it is like to be well!

And now for the last 3 weeks again only the way it has been in the worst times. The analysis wasn't making any progress—in any case I took an altogether refractory attitude against its curative influence. There were indeed better days in between—but they were never entirely lacking earlier either. Finally I had my doubts about the whole method. Not the theories of repression, etc. . . . but about the possibility of a lasting cure in all cases. Is all this only the last obstinate fight of the unconscious against getting well? Or is the transference to Dr. A. so strong that the subconscious wants to uphold this relationship at any price and so deploys the whole corona of old symptoms to show that I am still far from well, I must remain under treatment for a long time. Undoubtedly I enjoy going to the analysis and am happy in the morning when it occurs to me on my way to college that today I am to be there at quarter to 10 instead of 2 o'clock as usual. So what makes the analysis so indispensable to the subconscious? For one thing, the attachment to Dr. A. in itself. But above all: during that hour only I am, only I, undivided, the center of interest. I can talk about anything I ever felt and thought and know that it is being heard by another person. Also, I know that this spiritual disrobing, just as the physical undressing, gives the sensual pleasure of shy embarrassment and submission, and also that self-exhibition satisfies a strong sexual drive carried over from childhood.

From way back the urge to make myself interesting unquestionably dominated my relationship to people. This desire that others should pay attention to me, my singularity, is really the old exhibitionist tendency, but there is further an urge to martyrdom contained in it since one puts oneself forward just as much through one's bad as through one's good characteristics and must suffer for it; furthermore, the old childish "megalomania"; in short, one wants to be something quite special—and furthermore, a colossal need for an object, the need to please many people, to conquer many. If a few are taken in by this and make one feel that they consider one "a genius," the swindle is complete. There is nothing more unbearable than the thought of disappearing quietly in the great mass of the average, nothing more fatal than the reproach of being told one is a nice, friendly, average person. In order to stand out through achievement, however, one would have to work. Intellectual work is nevertheless thoroughly repugnant to the unconscious because it distracts it from its activity in sexual life. So one dabbles in "moods," one appears now gay, self-aware, competent, up-and-doing, and now burdened by a heavy passivity and fatigue, even playing with death wishes. Along this line the subconscious just incidentally profits in all sorts of ways. In states of exhaustion it can freely indulge its inclination to passivity. Then, when serious work is impossible, it can help itself in fantasies to everything life denies.

Am I then a quite simple case of hysteria? At least I know that I want him to have a scientific interest in me. The wish for a more personal love may well have been relegated to the less known realm of wishing.

The fantasy I had even before the analysis began clearly speaks for this: I pictured to myself the situation as it would be when Dr. A. asked permission to write up my case scientifically and publish it—this would obligate him to study all the expressions of my neurosis with a special, almost "affectionate" care, and in return for my being his subject of scientific research, he would treat me for nothing, nothing at all.

Thus from the very start my subconscious wanted to eliminate the purely professional element and set up a personal relationship in such a way that I was merely the *doctor's* object. Further: when I dreamed that my case history was to be published, that was simply exhibitionism on a grand scale.

The analysis, however, was of no overwhelming interest. I became obviously better—there was even a full week of the sheerest well-being, so that I was convinced the analysis was over, I was well. In that week Dr. A. was away. So I had no possibility of making myself interesting to him. Toward the end of that good period I heard that Karl U. was now almost through with his analysis. Idchen too was distinctly better. So I could only make myself more important in Dr. A.'s eyes by getting worse and thus showing him that he would not be done with me as quickly as with the others.

No different from the way I used to try to attract Frl. Banning's interest by being naughty; for his powerlessness in face of my condition worried him—and I knew it. Not satisfied with that, I repeatedly told him that I no longer had any confidence, that the analysis was doing me no good.

2 January 1911

If I am taking up my diary again it is from the ardent endeavor to master this illness at last. So much is better than it was before. The predominance of an equable, gay mood, the even tenor of my love for Oskar, and that of my capacity for sexual enjoyment, a definitely increased self-assurance in comparison to before, together with less shyness and less tendency to defensiveness toward others— those are undoubtedly new achievements. The really severe attacks of fatigue, too, belong to the past. Yet I still have to fight against fatigue a great deal, without doubt I need an abnormal amount of sleep and hence have little capacity for work. This is my greatest worry. Were it just a matter of the 2 or 3 hours of afternoon nap and the 10-hour rest at night—but that isn't the whole story: all the rest of the time I am not really fresh, tire quickly when studying so that I have to exert willpower repeatedly to keep on studying for my exam. On the other hand, I think I notice that this incapacity extends less than before to the area of other activities, so that there are fewer hours and days when I am useless for anything whatever. According to whether the freshness and ability to work are there or more or less lacking, I think of the work the future will bring me in family and profession with great joy or with trepidation and resistance. In the same way my self-confidence goes up or down accordingly.

Problems of self-confidence in my attitude toward other people constitute the other burden under which I suffer.

In this too there is no comparison with the past. But there are many indications that speak only too clearly for the existence of something that inhibits me. While Oskar enjoys getting to know a new person, especially when he approaches him with a prejudice in his favor, I am afraid of it, and in every case where the choice is up to me, I would prefer not to come in contact with him. This shyness is absolutely not accompanied by any idea that a new person couldn't mean anything to me—no, it is present even when, and perhaps particularly strongly when, the person in question has been described to me as outstanding in some respect or important or even just as a person of great self-assurance. Then, when after seeing the person in question several times I convince myself that he isn't so overwhelming after all, that he too is like other people, and that the indefinite fear I had of him has once more proved to have been unfounded, then an opposite tendency is apt to appear: namely that of underrating him. In any case, I tend to place him on an absolute scale of values for people that I am constantly trying to find. While Oskar simply takes a person as he is and in his great kindness lays more weight on the good in him with regard to his capacity for development than on the other, I am always quickly there with value judgments, trying to give opinions like "valuable" and "inferior" a definable or applicable content. Even with people I know, I avoid rather than seek association, here mostly with the idea that it is only a waste of time, nothing worthwhile would come of it. That this does in fact very often turn out to be so—at least from my point of view—is again in most cases my own fault. It is just as if I were afraid the conversation might go deep, especially that it might become too personal. A typical example of this was my attitude toward Frau H. I have a sincere sympathy for her, and at times when I longed to have a friend, I certainly thought she and I could be good friends. She has an open, simple, natural personality. She came to see me recently—and I managed to talk with her for 2 hours without our coming one bit closer. Apparently there was a repression there that brought about this behavior despite an honest wish to be close.

3 January 1911

Sonni doesn't shrink from the greatest discomforts for the sake of a sight of her once beloved Cousin Jochen.* She went into the Mausoleum and, full of ecstasy, kissed the old Kaiser's hand—a repetition of war-year doings in Bielefeld 1870 to 71, probably the sunniest time of her life, the time of her "great" love, her love for an officer who fell in the war. All the same symptoms: flight into a time when she was desirable and was desired. I had to think of myself. In these years of our marriage, until the analysis brought release from the repression, I could not free myself from my old loves, they exerted their old charm on me almost undiminished. My consciousness defended this state as loyalty, the perseverance of a once-given feeling. Now that my relation with Oskar has become sexually harmonious, these feelings are much reduced. I doubt that a man who once meant something sexually can ever lose his charm for us *totally*. The fact that no gratification had ever taken place would be apt to prevent this all the more.

I am not clear about my relationship to Losch. I am not conscious of any stimulus from his side. But various things make me distrustful: my frequently quite explosive dislike of Idchen, combined with the idea she is not worthy of him or with the faint suspicion that the pecuniary advantages she has to offer may contribute to her hold on him; my indignation at Idchen when from my point of view she treats Losch badly; and above all, occasional

---

* Little Jo, the Emperor Franz Josef. [Ed.]

dreams that offer an obvious interpretation. Unfortunately, I no longer remember much of my last night's dream.

4 January 1911

For the last 3 days my working capacity, while not over-powering, has yet been of a certain average steadiness. Instead of a long afternoon sleep in bed, I just lay down on the sofa for a short time. Also I wasn't tired particularly early in the evening. Where work is concerned, a rapidly growing fatigue sets in after some 10 minutes. Once I have conquered this, it usually goes very well and with fresh vigor. When I have been studying one subject for an hour or an hour and a half, a certain distaste and languor set in, my assimilative capacity lessens. This last symptom is probably psychological, because since studying for an exam always involves only receptive activity, one tires incomparably faster than one does in the productive activity. This is the case with Oskar, too. The first attack of fatigue must, on the contrary, depend on inner repressions. In what do these consist? Why are they not present when one is working productively? I really have almost never worked productively, and I am afraid of it, too. This fear comes from mistrust of my own capacity, perhaps also from the tendency Alfred Adler considers characteristic of neurotics: "Always wanting to be first, and not giving any credit to others." Or rather from both tendencies together: from a feeling of uncertainty and inferiority, I am afraid that I will not be able to do anything first class, above average, and therefore prefer not to attempt it at all, perhaps trying to create a special position for myself through this exaggerated refusal. Of course, the reproach I was always most anxious to avoid in any field was to be judged ordinary, average. Since, for example, I was in no position to shine through beauty, I wanted at least to look "interesting." If someone had said of me: she is ugly, yes, but looks uncommonly intelligent or whatever, I would not have taken that as a derogatory opinion. Furthermore Sonni is just like that. She has to be first everywhere, uses every available means to put herself in the foreground, make herself interesting: hence her craze for giving presents, her grand bearing, her desire to command in the house; hence her having managed to make me, even up to my 18th or 19th year, look upon her as perfection itself.

That is why so many hysterical people are delusive, because they do understand how to thrust their personality into a good, or anyway a striking, light. Perhaps this also gives rise to my fear of social gatherings, because I am afraid I won't be able to play first fiddle. In any case, it may be one of the reasons, for otherwise one simply goes to them calmly, moves in forms to which one is accustomed, and quite smoothly fits into the given situation. And probably hence, too, my disproportionate anxiety about exams: for example, I was, of course, quite sure of getting through graduation, at least I could have been—but probably I wanted to do particularly well, became anxious, nervous, and in consequence, when the exam actually came, unable to do anything. A person like Oskar consciously avoids receptive or mechanical work as far as he possibly can— with me, on the contrary, the state exam, for example, is not as unpleasant as the doctoral thesis. The same with Idchen. And perhaps with women in general more than with men. Adler says: "In fact the masculine protest is developed in every woman and makes her inwardly unfree." That means: every woman feels herself to be primarily, as such, inferior to men. The originates from a girl's strength being less than a boy's, and, according to Freud, from lack of a penis. Even with regard to her parents, a girl as a rule sees her father as the stronger, controlling partner, setting the tone. But she identifies early on with her mother. I know that as a child I wanted for a long time to be a boy, that I envied Berndt because he could stand near a tree and pee, that in charades I played a prince, that I loved to wear pants and was happy in my gym suit; perhaps hence also that at the age of 12 I cut my hair off to my neckline, thus being the curly haired prince again.

I didn't like small children at all: rejection of specifically feminine motherliness. Striking, however, is the intensity with which I played with dolls. So: a girl considers herself inferior and protests against that, i.e., she tries to adopt as many masculine characteristics as possible or to stand out in some other form. In school, for example, since she hasn't the physical strength. It was always my pride that in school I was better than Berndt, that there were more amusing childhood stories about me than about him. But the neurotic's every attempt at compensation leads to over-compensation; with the ever-present sense of inferiority goes the desire to stand out, and a hypersensitivity toward reprimand and reproach.

And out of all this: the inner constraint of a person who has something to hide from others. I want to conceal from myself and from others my feeling of inferiority—hence, I cannot simply give myself, naturally, just as I am, but am always on my guard against other people: only don't expose yourself, conceal your inferiority through excelling. Only people who give themselves without pretensions, just as they are, who cannot do otherwise than they do, have a beneficent influence on others.

5 January 1911

I am restless, excited, and my heart is beating fast. Sonni was here and told me that Anita's little boy has died. It was probably this that has affected me so. I know how attached she was to him. If the news has upset me so there must be an identification involved. I immediately had the wish to cry my heart out, and to press Tobby to me in the fear of losing him. I also had the idea that the exam is a less anxious matter than the baby,* because one can control it better and has it in hand, but the little one could be taken from me by a thousand things against which I am powerless. And yet the emotion seems to me too great for the occasion. Is there a repressed wish behind it: that my little one should die soon like Anita's? That I do not have this wish consciously, but am already experiencing an overflowing feeling of tenderness for the little creature, has nothing to do with it. What does the unconscious care about that? If something suppressed is involved here, it must surely be an idea that cannot become conscious, of which I would be ashamed in my conscious self or more likely would think myself incapable of. So what could my subconscious instinctual life have against the baby? For one thing, it imposes an inactivity of almost 3 months on marital intercourse. Then it disfigures me, makes me less desirable to other men; only not to Oskar, only to other men. If in addition the baby causes me to feel a stronger compulsion toward the monogamous relation, which always goes against the grain of the subconscious, it can all be summed up in one term: it is a repression of my prostitution drive. A person who has no children and never will can give herself to many men with much less punishment, no burdensome consequences come of it. Not enough that it restricts vagabonding, it imposes many duties that run

---

* She is by now six months pregnant. [Ed.]

counter to many pleasures, curtailing time for examinations and for continuing my education. I can travel only a little or with difficulty, I can't do all day what I want to do, but have strict duties I cannot shake. Perhaps it is going to be for me as it would be for a person who has always regulated the course of his day to suit himself and then comes into an institution where every hour is fixed by an authority. Won't he already feel in advance a secret resistance to and hatred of this authority? Isn't the baby a tyrannical authority of this sort that would rob me of my golden freedom? Something else occurs to me: with my present deep aversion to Sonni I may have a resistance against finding myself in a situation that makes me resemble her: becoming a mother, as she is my mother.

But of course the trouble may lie along the line of "masculine protest." Nothing is more specifically feminine than motherliness, but as I found myself inferior, being a feminine creature, and in consequence tried to be masculine, a situation that like no other keeps my femininity before my eyes and others' must be painful to me.

Then new duties loom in the raising of the child. With my uncertainty and lack of self-confidence I am afraid I may not be able to fulfill them. And reflect with death wishes on the being that is piling these duties upon me. It just occurs to me that at lunch I read a story in which a man, worried about being able to support his child, wished it dead and then, when it was rescued from an actual mortal danger, could not contain himself for joy. After lunch I was so tired that I slept soundly for a good 2 hours. So perhaps the news about Anita was just a cut in an old notch; perhaps I had already identified myself with that man in the thought: everything would be so much simpler—and more enjoyable—if the baby didn't come.

9 January 1911

On Saturday I was not very lively, on Sunday I tired easily all day and in the evening became very restive and anxious, so that I didn't want to be alone, and since Oskar was still working on his editorial, I installed myself on the sofa in his room. Last night a nightmare that I immediately forgot; I recall only that, in connection with a picture in *Die Jugend* ["The Last Judgment"], people were prodding and beating a man who was bound. Then this morning I could only be wakened with difficulty. And now I am totally incapable of concentrating my thoughts on work, have no desire to do so, am oppressed, feel a tightness in my throat, my heart is beating fast, and I feel chilly. Besides, I didn't really want to get at my diary but huddled idly for a long time by the stove, even after I had opened the diary with some effort and written the first sentence. From all this it is certainly to be concluded that something pathogenic has been accumulating in my subconscious and there are resistances against the solution.

One possibility that has just occurred to me is that Idchen told me the other day she wanted to go or had gone back to Dr. Abraham. For weeks I had been considering this possibility for myself, but then tried to progress with this self-analysis first. This wish has probably revived in me through Idchen's decision.

So for the last few days I have not written anything in the diary. I produced fatigue again, in order to induce myself to go back to Dr. Abraham for treatment. It may be that not only the personal transference relating to the wish for a new treatment played a role in this but also a certain jealousy of Idchen, who is with him now while I am not.

A second cause of illness is clear to me by its presence but not in its exact connection. It lies—as so often—in Sonni. Yesterday morning we found the enclosed advertisement* in the newspaper. Even though we at once thought of Sonni because of the wording, which would fit her very well, the suspicion became really serious through the way she reacted to our joking about it. She was distinctly embarrassed and untruthful. Said nothing like: "Let me see it," or "I read that too," which would undoubtedly have been her natural way.

Oskar and I talked about it for a long time afterward and in doing so I became apprehensive and restless. Recently Sonni had said several times jokingly: "You aren't doing anything at all to see that I find another husband, do get me one at an auction." It is easy to understand that her neediness has increased through Idchen and Losch living with her, through seeing our married happiness, and Berndt with his girls. As compensation she keeps stressing a congeniality between herself and Losch in contrast to Idchen, as for example: "Losch and I are, as so often, in complete agreement on this." Along with this it may also be that she very well sees her money will not hold out long if she goes on with her housekeeping as she does. Hence "wealthy gentleman" although this contradicts the "unselfish" in the advertisement and is not clever. As we discussed it, it seemed to us more and more probable that Sonni had perpetrated the advertisement, or certain at least that in reading it she identified herself with the writer and had deliberated whether to take similar action.

---

* "Accomplished, versatile, cultured elderly lady, unselfish, would like to provide for sunny twilight years of elderly or old, cultured, sensitive, wealthy gentleman needing care, through marriage. Discreet offer, ref. E.K. 579, publishing office this newspaper."

11 January 1911

Again things are not going well at all. A few errands yesterday overtaxed me out of all proportion. Am still lame in the legs today, have some pain in my back, eyes inflamed and sensitive. Fatigue. No question of work. My diary writing day before yesterday had no releasing effect whatsoever. In days like these the old fear comes back of this being a cyclical illness. I will really have to note down exactly how I am feeling each day to see whether regular periods alternate with each other. Then comes the question: is this periodic character connected with currents in the unconscious or is it something given, unchangeable, so that on the whole it can probably be mitigated through analysis but never eliminated by it? So that analysis could only have a releasing and beneficial effect if it fell, so to speak, in an ascending period?

12 January, evening

It is already half past 10, but I am not tired yet and would like so much to be awake when Oskar comes. I was really indignant today, at Idchen's unkindness to me, and only a glance at the little "Hannepeter" picture* cheered me up a little. That sweet little innocent child-face. It is a mistake for me to go to Idchen more often than absolutely necessary. Sonni and Idchen are both always annoying with their hysterics. Idchen just as much so on account of her inner attachment to her family. Losch is dear, it is true, and plays the piano beautifully, but his effect on me is ambivalent. On the whole the impression of disharmony there

---

* A painting of a small boy. [Ed.]

is depressing. Often, having gone there with pleasure, I have come away again dejected. So why go? It is obvious to me that on days when I feel perfectly well I instinctively stay away, while on bad days I often have the wish to go there. If I assume that the bad days are those on which I am under the command of my subconscious, then it must be subconscious tendencies that drive me to go there on those days, whereas on good days they are not strong enough to do so. These are probably directed mainly at Sonni. Perhaps I would be better off if she were not here. Wherever she is, she is always equally discontented—why should I, why should my baby, suffer from this? It is quite true: so long as she can have a pathogenic effect, I am not well. Although one must say that she has a depressing effect even on Hornvieh. Should I go to Dr. Abraham again? I think of it often, so it must be an agreeable idea. All the things one thinks of often when one lets one's thoughts wander are somehow pleasurable ideas, even if they don't seem so at first glance. In any case, they spring from such, and are perhaps conscious modifications of subconscious wishes. It often goes like this: deep down a wish stirs that is under strong censure. But it does come to the surface, mostly in a harmless form or slightly altered but with lightning speed, and is then further spun out in consciousness in a direction conscience allows. So when certain series of ideas occur repeatedly in, so to speak, an unsupervised conscious condition, one should make note of them.

One should go back again and search for the starting point of these ideas—or, if that is not successful, no direct solution being arrived at, the dreams themselves should be submitted to critical study. Perhaps this is particularly useful for self-analysis. Now, how fruitful a self-analysis can be anyway is an open question. I am inclined to doubt that a neurotic person would achieve his aim without outside help, such as books. The situation is different, of course, if the main resistances have been broken by a preceding analytic treatment; the main paths have been recognized, and one now has the inner freedom of movement to search out the whole terrain in detail from these main paths. Rolf taught me something in connection with this the other day. He had dreamt that he was in Walter S.'s house and Martha was not there. Walter came at him with a pistol. Rolf himself had quite correctly interpreted the adultery fantasy, but the homosexual fantasy in it, which struck me at first glance, he had not arrived at. Yet Rolf is, theoretically, clearly informed that every neurosis has its instinctive homosexual motives. That makes me wonder. With Rolf, to be sure, the need for causality is relatively quickly satisfied: when he has found a cause he sticks to it with a certain toughness and partiality, especially if it brings him any sort of pleasurable sensation.

18 January 1911

Feeling well yesterday afternoon and today. Worked. I got through everything quickly. Would like to get my general pathology done by February 1st. Until now haven't been able to carry out such an intention on account of variable capacity to work. Will it go all right now?

20 January 1911

Felt well and lively yesterday morning. Sonni was here for a long time, inveighing against Idchen and a thousand other things. None of her changes of mind or attitude surprise me any more, for all her arguments take on a kind of rigid monotony: that she is always putting herself aside, sacrificing herself, and yet people owe her *some* consideration, that she cannot stand people going to extremes, that Idchen is petty, common, and lets herself go, etc. . . . It was tiring, and from time to time I had to look at little "Hannepeter" to keep happy inside. Also that nobody needed her and that she found our coldness painful, was repeated over again.

In the afternoon a slight fatigue came over me; today it is so bad I can't work. All the old heaviness and weariness. Occasionally brief, well-localized pains in the epigastrium that make me think of stomach ulcers. Is this connected with Sonni again? But how? Yesterday I had the definite tendency to let everything slide off me and not let any complaints bother me. The affection Sonni demanded of me I gave with great inner reluctance. But in the end, of course, I cannot but sympathize with her and her fate, the fate of an aging woman who stands alone in the world without love, who has never had any gratification and is now morbidly seeking for expressions of affection from those nearest to her—insatiably—who doesn't know it is her discontent that never lets her rest and instead is always seeking satisfaction in external relationships that make her feel uncomfortable after a short while, who has a strong feeling for what she should be like and tries with every available means to maintain this fiction before herself and others, as if she really were like that, but in so doing becomes an almost intolerable burden to everybody.

23 January 1911

Day before yesterday I was tired in the morning and not able to work at all, wanted to give up completely. But stuck to it, although it went slowly and I had to read a lot of things 2 or 3 times before I grasped them. It was very exhausting. Gradually it went better. In the end it went splendidly, quickly, intensively, and made me happy. Then I became perfectly fresh, so that in the evening I even went along to the theater, to which Sonni had invited everybody in celebration of Losch's exam. All this, after not having been out in the evening for weeks. I was heartily amused too and even went along to the Rheingold. I didn't really want to go, but did not wish to upset the others by taking "Papa" [Oskar] away from them, a motive otherwise so very foreign to me. Got home about half past 1, not particularly tired. Wasn't tired at all yesterday either. Last evening Walter and Lisa came. It got very late, but I was fresh the whole time and even accompanied them as far as Roseneck Square between 12 and 1. I liked Lisa better than any woman I have met for a long time. She is unsophisticated, has an honest burning interest in all questions she comes up against, be it politics, child care, art matters, the woman question, the theater. Asked Oskar with great candor for information on whatever she wanted to know about and in which she considered him competent. In all a great capacity for deep sentiment and a general warm-heartedness. She again had a powerful effect on Hornvieh, so that in joke I pretended to be jealous. That I really was so, a short dream showed me, which I have completely forgotten. I only know that on waking I said to myself: so you really are jealous. During the night I was restless and could only go to sleep again in Oskar's arms. This morning I couldn't wake up at all and now feel battered and tired, incapable of anything. One should probably look for the cause in Lisa.

24 January 1911

Things finally went quite well yesterday after all. Working was difficult at first. But as I didn't give up, after a good hour I got well into the swing and accomplished something. Then I became generally fresh and happy. That would be "work therapy."

Oskar says it often happens to him that he can't get down to work for an hour or so. It pleased me very much to hear that, for then in my case it would only be a somewhat aggravated variety of psychological behavior. Today I am highly mobile and worked hard. Perhaps this time I will manage after all to finish what I have undertaken. That would be a satisfaction for me and increase my self-confidence. Then I can with great pleasure make a holiday of the days Agnes will be here. I do look forward to Agnes.*

Sunday it will be only 8 weeks till the baby comes. We haven't agreed on a name yet: Klaus, Gerhard, Jürgen, Hanspeter are at our disposal, and for a girl Ulrike. I'm to have a nurse too. Things should go well now! How happy I am. I always get annoyed when Sonni begins to "console" me, that I shall soon be released. It is just the expectation and the joy in it that are now so indescribably beautiful. And the feeling of carrying in me a small, becoming human being invests one with higher dignity and importance that makes me very happy and proud.

14 January February 1911

This is not the first time I have written "January" instead of February. I am much more apt to put down the wrong word with great regularity. No wonder. If we could turn

---

* Possibly her stepsister. [Ed.]

the clock back to a month ago, I would still have Sonni, all the dreadful things would not have happened yet.* Today is the first time I have felt the gloomy pressure diminish, for I am able to write in my diary again. Today for the first time there is a missing, a yearning, and not just the paralyzing horror at the incredibility of death.

I don't want to and can't yet write much, nor can I dissect the nervous symptoms that have re-established themselves with a certain completeness but with not nearly the old acuteness, the fatigue, the frigidity, my not at all looking forward to the baby and scarcely thinking about it—things will turn out all right and not be difficult to solve—only first one must let everything fade away and find the way back into living. Oskar dreamt last night that Sonni had risen from her deathbed and would spend two days with us, then she would have to die again. It is the wish to make good, to show her how much we loved her, to give her all the happiness in our power, in which we have failed so badly, so badly. Had we let her feel in her lifetime all the love that has now awakened in us so powerfully, how much happier she would have been.

15 February 1911

If I could go on working it would surely be better. I haven't even tried. I do only the more mechanical and pressing parts of the *Balneologische† Zeitung*—and otherwise am absolutely disinclined to do anything. Always want to sleep. This is probably an expression for my wishing I were dead like Sonni, and fatigue here is, at the same time, a being tired of life. The powerful instincts that bind one

---

* Her mother died on 2 February 1911. [Ed.]
† Balneology, the science of the therapeutic use of baths. [Ed.]

to life are now so weak in me, I have no drive to love, to motherhood, to work. That must mean: I don't want to have anything to do with life any more, I want to be dead with Sonni. There is not even a strong will in me to get well, I am resisting analysis; thus in this state of exhaustion and sleep, I come nearest to her condition, I want to keep it that way. As long as I do not feel a vigorous "*I will*" nothing really can be done. Yet more seems to be there today than yesterday. Shall probably be all there again soon. Otherwise Dr. Abraham will be my last refuge. But the very fact that today I am meditating about my getting well, and not about my grief, seems to bring me a step forward.

20 February 1911

It can't go on like this. I have too much to do, can't let one day after another pass by without having utilized it fully. I mustn't let myself be dominated by my distaste for everything. Oskar has found a very natural explanation for my behavior. It reveals the limitations of a self-analysis, for I did not arrive at it myself. It comes to this: Sonni's death in many respects means a release for me; I must have wished for it in many ways and greeted it with relief. For one thing, through her hysteria—which, furthermore, must have been increased and reinforced in these last years through organic changes in her vascular system—she gave us many an ill-humored hour. Her fate in the future lay before us as a threatening question to which we found no satisfactory answer, yet it repeatedly thrust itself upon us. Given Sonni's inability to handle money, the pecuniary side eventually became critical too, though it was not our chief concern. The main thing was that Sonni presented a constant danger to my health, and recurrences of poor health were often due—or in any case thought to be due—to her account. When she had her stroke a further consideration entered in: she would remain paralyzed and probably retain mental defects. Then it would have been our unavoidable duty to take her into our house and look after her. Our whole life would have been altered, a black shadow would have darkened our sunny, harmonious home. The thought was so dreadful to me that in those days I couldn't even think it through, but evaded it, either with the idea that Sonni could live alone with a nurse, or the thought that we would wait and see how things went, i.e., the wish that she might die before this question came up.

Then when death actually came, the consciousness of guilt for all these wishes that had previously been discreetly repressed came to the surface. I wanted to atone through an exaggerated grief, through torturing myself by reliving all the dreadful days of her sickness and death, through keeping away all distracting elements and all joy of life. The self-reproach for the countless unkindnesses one did her, large and small, the torment that this can never again be made good, this is a different, entirely conscious consciousness of guilt and would never by itself lead to nervous symptoms. It is a feeling of guilt that will always remain and that should teach me to become kinder toward the living. That is something which can make one serious but cannot be inimical to life, rather it must at bottom have an encouraging and ennobling effect on it. *Only guilt feelings toward repressed wishes have an inimical influence on life, restrictive, making for illness.*

21 February 1911

Yesterday things went very well again for the first time. I was active all day, got all sorts of things done: errands, signing up for exams, even worked hard for 2 hours on general pathology. With great freshness and a cheerful, serene mood. Last night I lay awake for a while, dreaming afterward that I was in the clinic to study. Three women lay dying. Two of them lay in 2 adjoining beds. They both looked already dead. The professor told us we should feel their hands; those of the woman on the right were already quite cool, those of the other hot. I stood by the bed of the woman on the right, thinking she was already dead. Then she moved her right hand once more and said: "thirsty," exactly as Sonni had done so often when she was in the hospital. When I awoke I felt heavy and tired—and still do. What does the dream mean? Now that I am no longer conscious of the self-torment in reliving the illness, does my subconscious not want to let it go? But what sort of sensual satisfaction would it have from that? Perhaps I am myself the woman on the left and am dying together with Sonni. For Sonni was my great childhood love. If the wish for her death was there on the one hand, on the other there was my strong love for her, which cannot let her go, and if she dies it wants to die too. The position of the beds, too, like those of a married couple, with me lying in the man's bed, would correspond with this interpretation. Indeed that must be it, this solution seems to me more and more likely.

10 April 1911

I see the last date and am surprised that it is so long since my last entry. And now meantime the baby is here, and my first childbed is behind me.

Brigitte born 29 March 1911.

11 April 1911

The nurse is gone now and I have my little one all to myself. All the corresponding work, too, naturally—but that will be all right. If only I were strong again and, above all, inwardly free. Abraham? Perhaps it would be good after all. He wrote, in a letter of congratulation, that he would like to visit me sometime. Now I am aware that whenever the doorbell rings, the thought shoots through my mind: it might be he. I don't quite understand the reason for this. So the readiness for transference is there in large measure—and on the other hand, it is just this that scares me about re-entering treatment; I think it will again bring up difficulties in arriving at solutions. But if, when recuperated, the state of my soul has not improved, I will go. The great load of work I shall have to surmount—baby, exams, newspaper, correspondence, psychotherapy report, diary, interpretation of my dreams—makes it imperative that I keep absolutely fit. Evidently I have a strong resistance against interpreting my dreams. For even if I put a sheet of paper for writing them down beside my bed, which mostly is not the case, I say to myself when I wake up: "I've already forgotten so much of that dream, it isn't worthwhile writing it down. I'll wait until I have remembered a complete dream." That this reason isn't valid I know well enough from theoretical instruction.

14 May 1911

Exhaustion after nursing. Nursing is a sort of autoerotic sensual satisfaction that like all stimuli of that kind produces sleepiness, cf. the various means for inducing sleep: sucking, slight stimulation of genitalia by pressure, position, indulging in fantasy, or chemical means. In nursing, such an intimate union of mother and child as never occurs later. Mutual sensual satisfaction; hence perhaps strengthening of the longing for one's own mother.

Motherliness—perhaps that is now the focal point of my interest, and that is why it struck me so profoundly when Oskar told me recently that what bound him so to Lisa was the fundamental kindness, the motherliness in her; she was like a little madonna; he often had the feeling he would like to lay his head in her lap and he would then be free of all sin. For if what I value most just now in a woman is motherliness, a remark like that was the very thing to arouse feelings of insufficiency. An afternoon nap is dangerous for me; it is as though one left the field to the enemy within. Autoeroticism, which can achieve the highest sensual satisfaction by itself, demands the closing off of the outer world. This closing off is most perfectly guaranteed by sleep. Sleep, dreams, fantasies need to be continued. Hence the difficult waking after an afternoon sleep; hence joy in work has gone to the devil again; one is tired. One wants to go on sleeping.

16 June 1911

What an incredibly rich and blessed time it will be when I am finished with the exam. Things are often pretty desperate now. No time for anything. Until today work has been going quite well, thanks to the self-analysis. Today bad again. Does that come from the Celtic saga? It was so horribly ghastly I thought I couldn't endure it as Oskar read it to me. Afterward that fear of death came again, the sudden certainty facing me, one day you most certainly must die. On healthy days this idea doesn't frighten me any more. Shouldn't I really go to Dr. Abraham again?

29 June 1911

After my afternoon sleep I woke up very tired. Incapable of work in the afternoon. Thought a lot about Oskar and wrote him an affectionate letter and had to weep a lot thinking of him, without really knowing why. It was the fear of losing him. Perhaps fear that he would now concentrate all his love on his mother,* as I had done with Sonni. Something of this sort sounded through in the letter —namely as renunciation. On my part, strong love or the will to it, the will to deepen our love.

[End of Diary]

[The following letter, evidently never sent, was found in the diary. We do not know whether Karen resumed analysis with Dr. Abraham.]

---

* She had died three days before, on 26 June 1911. [Ed.]

9 July 1911

My dear Dr. Abraham,

It is not going well at all. Won't I ever be getting well, completely well? I am beginning to despair of it. Most of the time it is not so bad, but I often feel as though I were paralyzed—there is a general disinclination in me. When I waken in the morning, I wish the day were already over. I still expect some relief once the pathology exam is over. Perhaps that is putting pressure on me. But I have no confidence in the influence of such rather external things. What else it can be is not clear to me. I am pretty well aware of what can happen theoretically and don't know of anything we have not repeatedly talked about in analysis. It is probably expedient to continue the analysis. If it suits you, I will come Saturday at 4—but I cannot say that I feel very confident. Of course the analysis has helped me unspeakably—but now I want more: to be perfectly well, to be able to work one day as well as another, above all to be able to depend on my state of health. This has not been the case up to now—and the whole second analysis did not really bring me any further. This exaggerated condition perplexes me. Perhaps I want to demonstrate this to you *ad oculos*? But if such motives can influence me, I just am not well yet. Otherwise the wish to continue the analysis could not have a pathogenic effect, and no positive or negative transference of any kind would have a decisive influence. So what more should we do in the analysis? Tread out old matters more broadly?

Or: does the real work not begin till *after* the analysis? Something like this: the analysis shows one one's enemies, but one must battle with them afterward, day by day. I was inclined to be satisfied with the theoretical understanding. But perhaps it is only meant to put the weapons into one's hands. Then the doctor would have to make his influence count in this direction, do more positive educational work. But I cannot force myself to work when I am tired. The power of my moral will is insufficient for that.

And I do so passionately want to be active. When I read over this letter I find it quite formless and, in part, offensive. If I do not send it off now, I will have a chance to show it to you in the analysis. So it might as well go. You will understand it correctly. Perhaps better than I myself. Furthermore, I expect no answer, in spite of the many question marks. I am coming myself. If Saturday does not suit you, I expect to hear from you. Otherwise it is not necessary. With best greetings,

Yours,
Karen Horney